ALGORITHMIC GOVERNANCE AND POWER

ALGORITHMIC GOVERNANCE AND POWER

How AI is Reshaping American Democracy

BY

NANCY S. LIND

Illinois State University, USA

emerald PUBLISHING

United Kingdom – North America – Japan – India
Malaysia – China

Emerald Publishing Limited
Emerald Publishing, Floor 5, Northspring, 21-23 Wellington Street, Leeds LS1 4DL

First edition 2026

British Library Cataloguing in Publication Data
A catalogue record for this book is available from the British Library

ISBN: 978-1-80791-659-6 (Print)
ISBN: 978-1-80791-658-9 (Online)
ISBN: 978-1-80791-660-2 (Epub)

Printed and bound by CPI Group (UK) Ltd, Croydon, CR0 4YY

INVESTOR IN PEOPLE

CONTENTS

PREFACE

As democracies worldwide grapple with the transnational power of digital platforms and the rapid deployment of artificial intelligence (AI), traditional models of governance are under unprecedented strain. The European Union has moved decisively: the AI Act (European Parliament & Council of the European Union [EU], 2024) establishes a risk-tiered regulatory regime for algorithmic systems across member states while the Digital Services Act imposes transparency and accountability obligations on major platforms. Meanwhile, jurisdictions from the United Kingdom to Brazil are debating analogous rules for governing algorithmic decision-making in public administration. The collision between technological infrastructure and democratic accountability has become a defining crisis of the current era—one that transcends any single legal tradition.

The American case is both constitutionally and institutionally distinct from those of other liberal democracies. The United States lacks a comprehensive federal AI statute comparable to the EU AI Act (EU, 2024). Its constitutional architecture—particularly the First Amendment protections that have extended to platform content moderation—constrains regulatory approaches that proceed more freely in other jurisdictions. Its administrative law tradition, now reshaped by the Supreme Court's 2024 decision in *Loper Bright*, imposes demands for explicit statutory justification at the precise moment when algorithmic governance makes such justification hardest to supply. Understanding the governance crisis in the American case requires engaging these specific constitutional and institutional conditions on their own terms, not simply importing models developed elsewhere.

Algorithmic Governance addresses this global technological shift by examining its uniquely American dimensions. It argues that the United States has entered the era of the hybrid state—a governance architecture in which public constitutional authority, private infrastructural power, and automated decision-making are inextricably linked. The pages that follow map that architecture, trace its consequences for democratic accountability and equal citizenship, and propose a legal and institutional framework for reclaiming democratic control. The Introduction develops the conceptual foundation for that argument.

BOOK ABSTRACT AND KEYWORDS

ABSTRACT

Algorithmic Governance and Power: How AI is Reshaping American Democracy examines the transformation of US governance from a visible, human-centered bureaucracy to a *hybrid state* dominated by algorithmic decision-making. As agencies deploy predictive tools and private platforms shape public discourse, conventional constitutional doctrines lag behind computational realities. This study traces how 21st century technologies collide with twentieth-century administrative law, focusing on the Supreme Court's 2024 overruling of *Chevron* deference (1984) in *Loper Bright Enterprises v. Raimondo* (2024), *Moody v. NetChoice* (2024), and *NetChoice v. Paxton* (2024). It reveals how opaque systems operationalize systemic inequality through *digital redlining*, embedding bias into code and eroding democratic visibility. Institutional power now circulates through data infrastructures, displacing human discretion and straining due-process safeguards. To meet this governance problem, the book proposes a legal and policy framework integrating algorithmic impact assessments, independent audits, and capacity-building reforms. These tools aim to tether distributed computational power to democratic accountability, transparency, and procedural fairness in the evolving architecture of the American state. The analysis advances the concept of infrastructural constitutionalism—that is, the embedding of constitutional principles such as due process, accountability, and transparency within the design and operation of computational systems, rather than solely within formal legal institutions, thereby relocating constitutional governance into the technical architecture of the state itself—as the governing principle for democratic accountability in the *hybrid state*.

Keywords: Algorithmic governance, administrative law, democratic accountability, digital platforms, digital redlining, microtargeting

INTRODUCTION: THE ARCHITECTURE OF THE *HYBRID STATE*

The United States is not the only democracy grappling with the rise of the algorithmic state—but it may be the most instructive one. Its constitutional architecture, its First Amendment constraints on platform regulation, its hollowed administrative capacity, and its Supreme Court's 2024 dismantling of the judicial deference doctrine that once absorbed technological ambiguity together make the American case the hardest test of whether liberal democratic institutions can govern computational power. What succeeds or fails here is likely to be diagnostic for every democratic system confronting similar pressures.

Traditional analyses of American government rely on a familiar and elegant map of power: the legislature makes the laws, the executive enforces them, and the judiciary interprets them. Around this constitutional triangle sit elections, political parties, interest groups, and the media—each playing a recognizable role in a system designed in the late 18th century and refined over two centuries of political development. It is a durable constitutional order, built upon the Madisonian mechanics of friction, checks, balances, and visible contestation.

It is also incomplete.

Today, many of the most consequential decisions shaping political life, economic opportunity, and civil liberties in the United States are not made solely in legislative chambers, executive offices, or courtrooms. They are made in spaces that the Constitution does not mention and that traditional legal doctrines struggle to regulate: within data infrastructures, within private digital platforms, and through automated computational processes that operate quietly but powerfully in the background of everyday administrative life. The crisis of the 21st century is not whether the state will govern through systems, but whether those systems will govern constitutionally.

This book is written for policymakers, regulatory professionals, and advanced students seeking to understand and govern the emerging architecture of algorithmic power. The premise of this book is that the wholesale transformation of American governance is no longer a looming horizon; it is an entrenched reality. We have crossed an epistemic threshold. From the allocation of public benefits and the deployment of predictive policing to the algorithmic curation of the public sphere and the microtargeting of the American electorate, the state has fundamentally changed how it sees and manages its citizens. To understand the future of American governance, we must map this new, hidden architecture. We must look beyond Congress and the courts to confront the rise of the *hybrid state*. Doing so requires engaging three adjacent literatures: revising theories of bureaucracy to incorporate technological discretion; reframing public–private relationships in terms of infrastructural power rather than regulatory hierarchy; and translating constitutional principles of reasoned decision-making into the operational logic of algorithms.

This book is situated at the intersection of four scholarly traditions, each of which it draws upon and, in turn, seeks to advance. The first is *critical public administration*—specifically the strand of that literature concerned with how bureaucratic discretion is exercised, delegated, and evaded: from Weber's rationalized hierarchy and Lipsky's street-level bureaucracy to Bovens and Zouridis's system-level pipelines. Against this tradition, the book argues that discretion has not merely been reorganized within bureaucracy but has migrated out of it entirely, into computational architectures that public administration scholarship has not yet fully theorized or constitutionally disciplined. The second is *institutional governance theory*—the comparative study of how authority is distributed across public and private actors, how accountability is maintained in complex principal–agent relationships, and how institutional arrangements shape and can be redesigned to check the exercise of power. The hybrid-state framework developed here extends that tradition by demonstrating that private digital infrastructure now performs governance functions that institutional theory has historically reserved for formally constituted public bodies, requiring a corresponding expansion of accountability doctrine. The third is *science and technology studies* (STS), which has long established that technical artifacts are not politically neutral and that the social and the technical co-produce one another. The book's theory of infrastructural constitutionalism is grounded in that tradition and argues that its insights must be translated into enforceable legal standards—into justiciable constitutional doctrine—if they are to function as governance instruments rather than remain critical description alone. The fourth is *democratic accountability scholarship*—the body of work that examines the conditions under which the exercise of public power can be made visible, contestable, and genuinely responsive to those it governs.

Against that tradition, this book argues that algorithmic governance generates an accountability deficit that conventional electoral, legislative, and judicial mechanisms are architecturally incapable of closing without the institutional redesign this book proposes. Taken together, these four traditions converge on a single diagnostic claim: when the machinery of governance changes fundamentally, the theory of democratic legitimacy must change with it. That is the animating conviction of every chapter that follows.

FROM INSTITUTIONAL AUTHORITY TO INFRASTRUCTURAL POWER

Classical accounts of American government assume that authority is exercised by identifiable human actors operating within formal, public institutions. In this traditional model, legislative intent is publicly debated and codified into statute, administrative action is justified through reasoned decision-making by human bureaucrats, and judicial review provides a mechanism of constraint and error correction. That entire model presupposes *visibility*. It assumes that when the state exercises power over an individual, the mechanisms of that power can be audited, explained, and legally contested.

Contemporary governance operates without this visibility. Decisions about political communication, economic opportunity, security risk, and social provision are now mediated through systems that are computational rather than deliberative, privately engineered rather than publicly authored, probabilistic rather than rule-bound, and opaque rather than inspectable. These systems do not sit outside the government; they are inextricably integrated into it. Federal and state agencies routinely rely on predictive machine-learning models and automated workflows to process millions of adjudications. Digital platforms govern the informational conditions under which democratic participation and electoral campaigns occur. Massive data infrastructures enable forms of behavioral targeting, surveillance, and classification that reshape electoral dynamics and administrative outcomes alike.

Power, in this technological environment, is no longer exercised solely through the holding of formal public office. It is exercised through control over the infrastructures that organize information, decision-making, and visibility. When a software engineer in a private technology firm decides how a risk-assessment algorithm weighs historical arrest data, or how a social media platform's recommendation engine amplifies political speech, they are performing functions that are inherently regulatory. They are writing the rules of this hybrid state in code rather than in law.

THE EMERGENCE OF HYBRID GOVERNANCE

Contemporary American governance is best understood as a hybrid system in which sovereign authority is heavily distributed. This digitally mediated governance rests upon three interlocking pillars:

- *Public Constitutional Authority:* The traditional institutions operating under constitutional and statutory constraints (agencies, courts, legislatures).
- *Private Infrastructural Power:* The technology firms, data brokers, and digital platforms that exercise quasi-regulatory control over civic communication, digital identity, and data flows.
- *Automated Decision-Making:* The algorithmic systems and machine-learning models that mediate human decision-making through encoded assumptions and statistical inference.

These domains do not operate independently; they are interdependent and mutually constitutive. Administrative agencies depend on privately developed proprietary systems to process their caseloads, effectively outsourcing sovereign discretion to commercial vendors. Platforms function as de facto regulators of public discourse, setting the boundaries of acceptable speech and algorithmic amplification. Courts are repeatedly asked to adjudicate disputes arising from processes that are technically complex, mathematically opaque, and fiercely resistant to traditional forms of legal scrutiny.

This hybridization deeply complicates the foundational concepts of political science and public law. The distinction between public authority and private action becomes dangerously unstable. Accountability is diffused across a web of actors with vastly differing incentives and legal obligations. Transparency is constrained not only by deliberate corporate secrecy and trade-secret protections, but by the sheer technical complexity of dynamic machine-learning models.

THE COLLISION OF LAW AND COMPUTATION: THE ACTIVE LEGAL BATTLEGROUND

Nowhere is the crisis of this hybrid state more apparent than in the collision between twentieth-century administrative law and 21st century computation. Modern public law was constructed around the assumption that the exercise of state power could be translated into reviewable reasons. *Algorithmic governance* relocates discretion upstream into the design of the system, creating a deep mismatch between the tools of governance and the law's capacity for oversight.

This tension is no longer abstract; it has become the defining judicial battleground of the current decade. With the 2024 overturning of *Chevron* deference in *Loper Bright*, the Supreme Court restored a much stronger, less deferential judicial role in statutory interpretation. This creates what this book identifies as the Loper Bright Opacity Paradox: the very moment courts demand more explicit justification from agencies is the moment agencies are least able to provide it. The full implications are developed in the law chapter.

This vulnerability is cascading through the federal courts. By expanding the statute of limitations for challenging agency actions, *Corner Post* (2024) expanded opportunities for litigation under *Loper Bright* (2024), allowing industry actors to aggressively challenge established privacy and data regulations. Lower courts are now forcing agencies into a doctrinally unstable "Shadow Skidmore" environment—as seen in strict, textualist rulings like *Chamber of Commerce of the United States of America v. Environmental Protection Agency* (2024) where relying on opaque algorithmic enforcement tools is no longer just bad policy, it is a concrete legal liability that invites judicial invalidation. Agencies must now defend their complex systems on the merits without a shield of broad deference, yet their actions are shaped by *black box* algorithms that resist straightforward explanation.

The private pillar of digitally mediated governance is leveraging constitutional protections to insulate itself from regulation. In the landmark *NetChoice* cases (*Moody v. NetChoice* and *NetChoice v. Paxton*), the Supreme Court vacated and remanded the lower court rulings without issuing a definitive substantive holding, finding that the courts below had failed to conduct a proper facial First Amendment analysis. The majority opinion by Justice Kagan and Justice Barrett's concurrence reveal a Court visibly struggling to categorize artificial intelligence (AI). To govern platforms without violating the First Amendment, regulators must now pursue "content-agnostic" algorithms—targeting the technical architecture of virality and data harvesting rather than dictating substantive speech.

Caught in this legal vice, this hybrid state demands an entirely new legislative response. Establishing technical standards alone is insufficient without explicit Congressional delegation. The path forward requires hardwiring algorithmic accountability directly into the law, bridging the gap between emerging bills like the Algorithmic Accountability Act (H.R. 5511, 2025), and the necessity of a modernized Digital Administrative Procedure Act (D-APA).

A clarification is warranted about this book's analytical relationship to Loper Bright. The Supreme Court's 2024 decision receives sustained attention throughout these pages not because administrative law doctrine is the book's central subject, but because Loper Bright is the catalyst that transforms what might otherwise be a normative complaint about algorithmic opacity into a live constitutional crisis. The decentralization of infrastructural power traced in this book—from agencies to private vendors, from deliberate human choice to encoded statistical inference—would be troubling even in a world of strong Chevron deference. But Loper Bright converts that systemic problem into an acute legal vulnerability: courts now demand the kind of transparent, statutory reasoning that algorithmic systems are architecturally incapable of supplying. The Loper Bright Opacity Paradox is therefore the juridical expression of the infrastructural power problem, not a separate doctrinal inquiry. Readers whose primary interest is in platform governance or electoral data will find the doctrine recede appropriately in those chapters; it returns with force in the administrative law and accountability chapters because that is where the paradox bites hardest.

THE CODIFICATION OF INEQUALITY

Beyond the separation of powers and the shifting doctrines of the courts, this hybrid state alters the social contract and the distribution of equality. While automated systems and data-driven pipelines are frequently sold to public agencies on the promise of objective, bias-free efficiency, the reality is far more perilous. These opaque systems operationalize and reorganize structural inequality through code.

When public and quasi-public systems rely on historical data, they inevitably reproduce the hierarchies of the past. Bias in training datasets yields unequal outcomes, as variables like zip codes, employment gaps, or prior law enforcement contact serve as proxies for race, class, and geographic disadvantage. This phenomenon, often termed digital redlining, reroutes historical exclusion into new, highly sterilized technological channels. What makes digital redlining so powerful is its invisibility. Because automated systems feed on the outputs of earlier institutions—generating new outputs that become the data for later rounds of governance—they create self-reinforcing feedback loops. Embedded inequality hardens into the operating logic of the state itself, functioning largely outside the traditional mechanisms of anti-discrimination law, which was built to catch intentional human animus, not statistical proxy bias optimized by a machine.

REFRAMING DEMOCRATIC PRINCIPLES

The normative implications of this sweeping transformation are severe. Democratic governance rests on the unyielding principles of accountability, transparency, due process, and equal representation. Each of these principles is currently buckling under the weight of conditions where decision-making authority is distributed across institutional and noninstitutional actors; where the logic of adjudication is buried in mathematical models that are difficult to interpret; and where citizens' information environments are personalized, fragmented, and algorithmically curated for commercial engagement rather than civic deliberation.

These are not abstract or academic concerns. They dictate concrete, life-altering outcomes: the allocation of housing and medical benefits, the duration of a prison sentence, the patterns of neighborhood surveillance, the exposure to political disinformation, and the distribution of economic opportunity across vulnerable populations. It is vital to acknowledge that technological systems offer genuine and necessary advantages. The scale of the modern American public sector demands efficiency. Automated systems possess the capacity to process complexity beyond human capability, clearing bureaucratic backlogs and identifying insights that human administrators might miss. The imperative, therefore, is not one of Luddite resistance, but of urgent institutional adaptation.

Understanding this monumental shift is essential for anyone seeking to make sense of contemporary policy, but it is doubly essential for those who must shape its future. Because if the machinery of government is changing—and it undeniably is—then the question is not simply how it works, but who it works for, and under what rules. Power in contemporary American government is exercised not only through institutions and constitutional law, but through control over data, systems, and informational infrastructures.

The question is no longer only how government is organized. It is how governance is produced. The algorithmic state is here; the task of the 21st century is to make it accountable to the people it governs.

The analysis that follows opens several lines of inquiry that subsequent scholarship should pursue. The hybrid-state lens generates important new research trajectories. Future work should empirically map how algorithmic systems redistribute discretion within and across institutions—examining, for instance, how agency procurement decisions or vendor architectures shape outcomes in welfare, policing, or immigration. Scholars may also explore comparative constitutional responses: how different legal traditions—European, East Asian, or Global South—mediate the tension between computational governance and democratic accountability.

Furthermore, interdisciplinary research is needed to bridge administrative law, computer science, and civic technology design, translating due process norms into concrete technical standards for explainability, documentation, and contestability. Finally, the hybrid-state paradigm invites a normative research agenda: not simply how to constrain algorithmic power, but how to imagine forms of algorithmic governance that strengthen democratic participation—systems that make citizens co-producers, not passive data subjects, of administrative knowledge.

A particularly urgent research trajectory concerns the transition from algorithmic scoring tools to autonomous AI agents—systems capable not merely of recommending but of initiating, delegating, and completing multi-step administrative actions without a discrete human decision point. Prominent AI researchers have characterized this as a shift from tools that augment human cognition to agents that substitute for human agency across entire workflows (Russell, 2019; Wooldridge, 2009). For constitutional purposes, this shift is not merely technical; it threatens to dissolve the "material influence" standard developed in this book's due process chapter, because agentic systems may produce legally consequential outcomes through cascades of micro-actions that no individual actor expressly authorized. The governance implications of multi-agent systems operating inside federal procurement, benefits adjudication, and law enforcement—systems that can task other systems—represent the next frontier of the hybrid-state problem.

The book's theory of infrastructural constitutionalism is also in substantive conversation with the tradition of STS, a body of scholarship that has long argued that technical artifacts are not politically neutral. Langdon Winner's foundational essay demonstrated that systems can embody authority relationships and reinforce power asymmetries independent of any individual designer's intent (Winner, 1980). Sheila Jasanoff's concept of sociotechnical imaginaries—the collectively held visions of social order that co-produce and are co-produced by scientific and technological projects—illuminates why algorithmic governance does not simply impose neutral efficiency but enacts a particular vision of administration as quantification (Jasanoff & Kim, 2015). Lucy Suchman's critique of plans-and-situated-action is equally relevant: the assumption embedded in automated systems that human situations can be fully anticipated and encoded in advance systematically underestimates the contextual judgment that administrative fairness requires (Suchman, 2007). By engaging these traditions, *Algorithmic Governance* locates the legal and constitutional argument within the broader sociotechnical critique of computational reason.

1

FROM BUREAUCRACY TO THE ALGORITHMIC STATE

Of the three pillars of the hybrid state identified in the Introduction, the first—automated decision-making within public agencies—has the deepest institutional roots. Its emergence required dismantling the human-centered bureaucracy that governed American administration for most of the 20th century. Decisions that shape people's lives—whether they receive benefits, how police are deployed, or how risk is assessed—are not made solely by identifiable public officials. They are produced through systems: data infrastructures, automated processes, and predictive models. These systems do not sit outside government; they are woven into it.

This chapter argues that American governance is undergoing a fundamental shift away from human-centered, street-level bureaucracy (Lipsky, 1980) toward system-centered, algorithmic decision-making. This transformation does not replace traditional institutions, but it changes how they function, how authority is exercised, and how accountability is maintained.

WEBER'S BUREAUCRACY: THE ORIGINAL LOGIC OF ADMINISTRATION

The modern administrative state is rooted in the work of Max Weber, who identified bureaucracy as the most rational and efficient form of organization for complex societies. Weber's model emphasized hierarchy, specialization, rule-bound decision-making, and impersonality (Weber, 1978). In this system, legitimacy derived from procedure. Officials did not rule arbitrarily; they applied general rules to cases. Decisions were expected to be consistent, predictable, and grounded in expertise.

In the United States, this model shaped the expansion of administrative agencies throughout the 20th century. From New Deal programs to postwar regulatory bodies, governance relied on professional bureaucracies. Yet Weber's model contained an inherent tension: rules do not interpret themselves. Bureaucrats must apply them, and in doing so, they exercise discretion.

STREET-LEVEL BUREAUCRACY AND THE PROBLEM OF DISCRETION

Michael Lipsky's concept of street-level bureaucracy highlighted the importance of frontline decision-makers in shaping policy outcomes. Police officers, social workers, and case managers effectively make policy through their daily decisions (Lipsky, 1980). This insight reframed administration as a site of power rather than mere implementation. It also exposed several persistent deficiencies:

- Variation in decisions across similar cases.
- Implicit bias influencing outcomes.
- Resource constraints shaping behavior.
- Limited oversight of individual discretion.

By the late 20th century, critics argued that bureaucratic discretion undermined fairness and efficiency. Governments faced growing pressure to standardize decision-making processes. As Bovens and Zouridis (2002) observed, administrative systems began shifting from "street-level" to "system-level" bureaucracies, where decision-making is built into information systems rather than exercised directly by individuals.

THE DIGITAL TURN IN GOVERNANCE

The rise of computing technologies transformed administrative capacity. Early systems focused on record-keeping, but advances in data processing enabled governments to analyze patterns, predict outcomes, and automate decisions. This shift accelerated in the 21st century with the growth of big data and machine learning.

Governments began adopting tools capable of processing vast datasets and generating recommendations or decisions at scale. Algorithmic governance refers to this emerging model in which decision-making authority is mediated by computational systems (Danaher et al., 2017). These systems offer clear advantages:

- Efficiency in processing large volumes of cases.
- Consistency across decisions.
- Data-driven insights.

They also introduce new forms of power that are less visible and more difficult to contest.

DECISION PIPELINES: HOW THE ALGORITHMIC STATE WORKS

Algorithmic governance operates through decision pipelines, which transform inputs into outputs through structured processes. A typical pipeline includes:

- Data collection (e.g., income, criminal history).
- Data processing and modeling.
- Risk scoring or classification.
- Decision output.

These decision pipelines are the operational core of the algorithmic state. They can either support human decision-making or replace it. In either case, they reshape the locus of discretion. Rather than occurring at the moment of decision, discretion is embedded earlier—in the design of the system. Choices about data, variables, and model construction determine outcomes in ways that may not be visible to end users. This shift represents a redistribution of power from frontline officials to system designers and institutional decision-makers.

CASE STUDY: BENEFITS ELIGIBILITY SYSTEMS

Public benefits administration illustrates the transformation from human discretion to automated decision-making. Historically, caseworkers determined eligibility by applying statutory criteria to individual circumstances. Today, integrated eligibility systems automate much of this process.

These systems improve efficiency but reduce flexibility. They apply rules uniformly, limiting the ability of caseworkers to account for context. Virginia Eubanks (2018) documents how automated welfare systems can produce exclusionary outcomes, particularly for marginalized populations. Applicants may be denied benefits based on data inputs without clear explanations. This raises concerns about procedural fairness. Individuals may struggle to understand or contest decisions made by automated systems. The shift from human judgment to system-generated outcomes represents an institutional change in how administration works.

CASE STUDY: PREDICTIVE POLICING

Predictive policing systems use historical crime data to forecast future crime patterns. Law enforcement agencies use these predictions to allocate resources. While presented as neutral and objective, these systems reflect underlying data patterns. Richardson et al. (2019) argue that predictive policing can reinforce existing inequalities by directing attention to already over-policed communities. This creates a feedback loop: increased policing generates more data, which reinforces predictions of risk. The result is not simply more efficient policing, but a reconfiguration of how policing decisions are made. The same embedded logic—discretion embedded in design, bias encoded in data—is visible in criminal risk assessment.

CASE STUDY: RISK ASSESSMENT AND COMPAS

Risk assessment tools represent another form of algorithmic governance. The COMPAS system, widely used in US courts, generates risk scores predicting recidivism. These scores influence decisions about bail, sentencing, and parole. Angwin et al. (2016) found that COMPAS produced racially disparate outcomes, raising concerns about bias. Berk et al. (2021) note that debates over fairness in such systems reflect broader tensions between statistical accuracy and normative equity.

The legal system has struggled to address these issues. In *State v. Loomis* (2016), the Wisconsin Supreme Court upheld the use of COMPAS while acknowledging its limitations. This case illustrates a key deficiency:

traditional law is not well equipped to evaluate algorithmic decision-making. If discretion has migrated into systems, the legal system must now confront not only agency reasoning, but system design itself.

CASE STUDY: BENEFITS ELIGIBILITY AND ALGORITHMIC DUE PROCESS: POST-2023 DEVELOPMENTS

The Medicaid unwinding that unfolded across 2023 and 2024 offers one of the most consequential recent illustrations of algorithmic governance failure at population scale. When pandemic-era continuous enrollment protections ended and states resumed regular eligibility redeterminations, the consequences were severe. More than 20 million Medicaid enrollees were disenrolled during the postpandemic unwinding period, according to analyses by the Centers for Medicare & Medicaid Services (CMS, 2024). A substantial share of those disenrollments resulted from procedural and administrative failures, including renewal barriers, documentation problems, incorrect notices, and automated eligibility-system errors in some states, rather than confirmed ineligibility. This figure should therefore be treated as the total disenrollment scale, not as proof that all coverage losses were caused by artificial intelligence (AI) or algorithmic error. The stronger and more defensible claim is that the unwinding exposed how procedural complexity, automated renewal systems, vendor-administered eligibility platforms, and weak notice-and-appeal safeguards can combine to produce large-scale administrative harm. This is not a due process failure at the margins; it is the black box problem operating at the scale of a national program, in real time, with immediate consequences for the health and housing stability of tens of millions of people.

The Texas case illuminates the vendor accountability dimension with particular clarity. Texas's automated benefits verification system—developed by multinational consulting firm Deloitte—produced extensive and repeated operational failures, including incorrect notices, wrongful denials, and lost documentation, trapping eligible applicants in cycles of reapplication while their circumstances deteriorated (National Health Law Program et al., 2024; Liss & Pradhan, 2024). Robert Austin, a single father in El Paso who was homeless with his young daughter when he applied for benefits, spent two years bouncing between reapplications as the system repeatedly lost or rejected his documentation—ultimately losing his car and relying on strangers for money to purchase diapers for his toddler (Parshley, 2025). The same systemic failure appeared independently in Colorado: a September 2023 statewide performance audit of Colorado's Medicaid correspondence system found at least one problem in 90% of sampled notices, including non-compliant dates and missing required elements—deficiencies the auditors noted had also appeared in prior 2016 and 2020 reviews (Colorado Office of the State Auditor, 2023). That system was also administered under a Deloitte contract (Liss & Pradhan, 2024). The recurrence of identical failure modes across two states under the same vendor points not to implementation error but to procurement architecture—a condition in which the design logic of a private contractor becomes, in effect, the operating logic of state governance.

The due process implications extend beyond the rate of erroneous denials to the procedural dynamics of the appeal process itself. An April 2025 report by the National Academy of Social Insurance found that at the initial disability determination stage, 48% of Social Security disability denials that are appealed are allowed—and that a substantial share of applicants who would qualify drop out of the appeals process entirely before receiving a determination (National Academy of Social Insurance [NASI], 2025). The error rate matters, but the attrition rate matters more: a system that produces reversible errors generates constitutional injury not only when it denies benefits, but when it does so in ways that systematically discourage the assertion of appeal rights by the most vulnerable claimants.

Michigan's automated unemployment fraud detection system offers a categorically distinct but analytically related failure mode. Fields-Meyer and Hertel-Fernandez (2024) report that when Michigan deployed its automated unemployment fraud detection system—widely known as Michigan Integrated Data Automated System (MiDAS)—it identified fivefold more fraud than the prior system, generating accusations against approximately 40,000 individuals who had not committed fraud. A class action lawsuit resulting from these wrongful accusations was settled in 2024; the State of Michigan reached a $20 million agreement with approximately 3,200 class members who had been falsely accused of fraud between 2013 and 2015 (Michigan Department of Attorney General, 2022, 2024). Michigan's Court of Claims granted final approval of that settlement on January 29, 2024 (Michigan Department of Attorney General, 2024; *Bauserman v. Unemployment Insurance Agency*, 2019).

The analytic significance of this case lies in how the system's failure was initially perceived. A detection rate five times higher than the prior system was treated internally as evidence of the algorithm's superior effectiveness—when in fact it reflected a fundamental miscalibration of sensitivity, generating false positives at a rate that could not have passed meaningful human review.

The cost of that miscalibration was borne entirely by claimants: in reputational damage, legal entanglement, and the administrative burden of proving the negative. The state bore no equivalent cost for the error.

Together, these cases establish what the COMPAS and predictive policing literature documented in criminal justice: a consistent asymmetry in which algorithmic error is systematically offloaded onto the most vulnerable parties to the administrative relationship while remaining invisible to, and uncontested within, the systems that produced it.

LAW CONFRONTS THE ALGORITHMIC STATE

Administrative law has long provided the primary body of doctrine for regulating bureaucratic decision-making. A major doctrine in this area is *Chevron* deference, established in *Chevron USA, Inc. v. Natural Resources Defense Council, Inc.* (1984). *Chevron* held that courts should defer to reasonable agency interpretations of ambiguous statutes. This doctrine recognized agency expertise and reinforced the role of the administrative state.

The Loper Bright Opacity Paradox, introduced above, is no longer theoretical. When decisions are built into technical systems, the question is no longer only how agencies interpret statutes, but how systems implement them. This tension came to a head in *Loper Bright* (2024), where the Supreme Court rejected *Chevron* (1984) deference. The decision signaled a shift toward greater judicial authority over administrative interpretation.

The implications for algorithmic governance are direct and far-reaching. As courts take a more active role, they may be asked to evaluate not only agency interpretations, but also the systems through which those interpretations are implemented.

THE BLACK BOX PROBLEM

In administrative settings, this opacity manifests as an inability to trace how specific outputs are generated, complicating both review and appeal. Pasquale (2015) argues that this opacity limits judicial review by preventing meaningful oversight. Individuals affected by decisions may not understand how those decisions were made. This is particularly problematic in government contexts, where transparency is a core democratic value. The problem is not simply technical, but political: how to reconcile complex systems with the need for public accountability.

EFFICIENCY, EQUITY, AND DEMOCRATIC VALUES

Algorithmic systems promise efficiency, but they also raise concerns about equity. O'Neil (2016) demonstrates how data-driven systems can reinforce inequality, particularly when they rely on biased data. Human decision-making is not inherently fair. The question is not whether to use algorithmic systems, but how to design and regulate them. This requires balancing competing values:

- Efficiency versus fairness.
- Consistency versus flexibility.
- Innovation versus accountability.

THE EMERGING ALGORITHMIC STATE

The transition from bureaucracy to the algorithmic state represents a shift in the architecture of governance. In practice, this shift becomes visible in how decisions are produced—through structured decision pipelines rather than individual judgment. Understanding this shift is essential for analyzing modern American government.

The algorithmic state represents an inversion of Max Weber's original bureaucratic vision. Where classical bureaucracy relied on visible, rule-bound procedures applied by accountable human officials, hybrid governance writes its rules into opaque computational pipelines. Discretion has not been eliminated, as Lipsky might have feared; it has been relocated from the street-level bureaucrat to the system architect. This chapter demonstrates how that broader systemic shift—introduced in the Introduction—operates inside administrative agencies. The transformation described in this chapter raises a critical question: who controls the rules governing these systems? For much of the 20th century, the answer lay in administrative agencies, supported by judicial deference under *Chevron* (1984). But as courts reconsider that deference—culminating in *Loper Bright* (2024), the balance of power is shifting.

Because automated systems relocate discretion from visible frontline workers to invisible system architects, agencies cannot govern what they have not mapped. Computational pipelines must be formally documented and published as a condition of deployment—not as an afterthought. System architecture should be treated as a policy decision in its own right, requiring impact assessments before procurement rather than audits after harm. And federal and state contracts must explicitly prohibit the trade-secret shields that currently allow vendors to operate inside public administration without public accountability. The full institutional design for these measures is developed in the final chapter; what the evidence in this chapter establishes is their necessity.

2

PLATFORMS AS POLITICAL INSTITUTIONS

If discretion has migrated from human bureaucrats to algorithmic systems within public agencies, an equally consequential migration has occurred beyond the formal boundaries of government—into private platforms, where power now operates outside traditional public administrative authority. Within this hybrid state, power is not exclusively governmental; private technology platforms now function as parallel political institutions that govern the informational conditions under which democratic participation occurs. These platforms—operated by companies such as Meta Platforms, Google, and X Corp.—have become the primary venues through which citizens encounter political information.

What distinguishes platforms from earlier media institutions is not simply their scale, though that scale is unprecedented. It is their capacity to configure information environments dynamically, continuously, and at the level of individual users. Rather than presenting a fixed set of content to a broad audience, platforms curate personalized streams of information shaped by algorithmic systems and user data. In doing so, they determine not only what information exists in a public sense, but what information is seen.

This institutional shift has implications for political visibility, as decision-making is no longer governed solely by public institutions or traditional media gatekeepers. Instead, it is mediated by systems designed and operated by private actors.

Scholars have recognized that this shift requires a conceptual reorientation. Platforms are not merely communication tools or neutral intermediaries; they must be understood as part of the broader architecture of governance.

This chapter develops that argument in three stages. First, it examines how platforms operate as agenda-setters, shaping the issues that dominate public discourse. Second, it analyzes content moderation as a form of governance that parallels constitutional principles, particularly those associated with the First Amendment. Third, it explores the controversies surrounding deplatforming and the question of democratic legitimacy. Together, these developments point to a strong conclusion: platforms exercise power that is political in substance, even if it is not formally governmental in form.

PLATFORMS AS AGENDA-SETTERS

Agenda-setting has long been a foundational concept in political science, traditionally associated with the role of mass media in shaping public priorities. In the digital age, this function has been transformed by platforms that do far more than select headlines or frame stories. They construct entire informational ecosystems.

Platforms determine what users see through complex ranking systems that prioritize certain types of content over others. These systems rely on a variety of signals, including engagement metrics, user behavior, and inferred preferences. The result is a highly individualized experience in which each user encounters a different version of political reality.

This personalization distinguishes platforms from traditional media in two critical ways. First, it fragments the public sphere. Instead of a shared set of issues and narratives, users encounter divergent streams of information. Second, it intensifies the influence of platform design. Because visibility is mediated through algorithms, small changes in ranking systems can have large effects on what information becomes prominent.

Research has shown that algorithmic systems can significantly influence exposure to political content, shaping not only what users see but how they interpret it (Tufekci, 2014). These effects are often indirect and difficult to detect, making them harder to regulate or contest.

Importantly, platforms do not operate in a vacuum. Their agenda-setting function is shaped by commercial incentives. Engagement-driven models reward content that generates attention, which can include emotionally charged or polarizing material. This creates a structural bias toward certain types of content, even in the absence of explicit editorial intent.

Platforms retain the ability to intervene directly. They can promote authoritative sources, demote misinformation, or remove harmful content. These interventions further reinforce their role as agenda-setters. The result is a system in which platforms automate and curate political visibility. They do not simply reflect public discourse; they shape it.

FROM MEDIA COMPANIES TO POLITICAL INSTITUTIONS

To understand the significance of platform power, it is necessary to move beyond analogies to traditional media. While platforms share some characteristics with media organizations, their role in political life is broader and more deeply entrenched.

Traditional media organizations act as intermediaries between events and audiences. They select, frame, and disseminate information, but they do not typically control the underlying infrastructure of communication. Platforms, by contrast, operate at the level of infrastructure. They provide the environment within which communication occurs.

This infrastructural role gives platforms a form of authority that resembles that of political institutions. They establish rules governing participation, enforce those rules through moderation systems, and shape the conditions under which public discourse takes place. Unlike governments, platforms are not formally accountable to citizens. Their authority derives from ownership and contractual relationships with users rather than democratic processes. Yet their decisions have consequences that are indistinguishable from those of public institutions in key respects.

This hybrid status has led scholars to characterize platforms as "private governors" or "infrastructure institutions" (Gillespie, 2018; Pasquale, 2015). These terms capture the idea that platforms exercise regulatory power over social and political activity, even though they operate outside traditional governmental institutions.

The institutionalization of platform power is also evident in their interactions with other actors. Governments rely on platforms to disseminate information and enforce policies, while political campaigns depend on them for communication and mobilization. This interdependence further blurs the line between public and private authority.

Understanding platforms as political institutions does not mean equating them with governments. Rather, it means recognizing that they perform governance functions that must be analyzed alongside traditional institutions.

CONTENT MODERATION AS GOVERNANCE

Content moderation is the primary mechanism through which platforms exercise their institutional power. It involves the creation and enforcement of rules that govern user behavior and the circulation of information. These rules are typically articulated in platform policies, such as community standards or terms of service. They define categories of prohibited or restricted content, including hate speech, misinformation, and incitement to violence. They also establish procedures for enforcement, including removal, demotion, and account suspension.

In practice, content moderation operates as a regulatory system. It sets norms, applies them to individual cases, and imposes sanctions for violations. This process closely parallels traditional forms of governance, even though it is carried out by private entities.

The scale of moderation adds another layer of complexity. Platforms must process vast amounts of content, making it impossible to rely solely on human review. Consequently, they use automated systems to detect and act on potential violations (Gillespie, 2018). These systems introduce new vulnerabilities. Automated moderation can be faster and more consistent than human review, but it is also prone to error and lacks contextual sensitivity. Decisions may be difficult to explain or appeal, raising concerns about fairness and accountability.

Moreover, moderation decisions often involve inherently political judgments. Determining what constitutes misinformation, for example, requires assessing the credibility of sources and the validity of claims. These are not purely technical questions. Content moderation functions as a form of governance that blends technical processes with normative judgments. It is both a system of rules and a site of political decision-making.

CONTENT MODERATION AND THE FIRST AMENDMENT

The rise of platform governance has prompted renewed attention to the First Amendment, particularly its application to private actors. Under traditional doctrine, the First Amendment restricts government action, not private conduct. Platforms, as private companies, are generally free to regulate speech on their services.

In both landmark *NetChoice* cases (*Moody v. NetChoice*, 2024; *NetChoice v. Paxton*, 2024), the Supreme Court addressed state laws that sought to limit platforms' ability to remove content. Rather than issuing a definitive substantive ruling, the Court unanimously vacated and remanded the cases, noting that the lower courts had failed to properly conduct a facial First Amendment analysis. The majority opinion and Justice Barrett's concurrence revealed unresolved judicial questions about automated systems. Barrett's concurrence agreed with vacating and remanding but objected to the majority's methodology: she argued that a proper facial challenge analysis requires examining a law's full range of applications across concrete cases, a standard the lower courts had not met, and that the majority's venture into First Amendment merits was therefore premature given the underdeveloped factual record—leaving unresolved how courts should classify AI-driven algorithmic curation as protected expression or regulable conduct. Alito's separate concurrence was a sharper substantive critique: he questioned the majority's foundational premise that platform content moderation constitutes protected editorial discretion comparable to traditional editorial judgment, objecting not merely to the timing of the Court's analysis but to the analytical approach the majority deployed in reaching it.

This fracture creates a crucial constitutional opening for digitally mediated governance: the "content-agnostic approach" carve-out. If regulators can target the underlying architecture of a platform—such as the speed of algorithmic amplification or the use of behavioral data for targeting—without dictating substantive speech outcomes, they may successfully bypass the First Amendment shield that otherwise protects platform moderation.

This recognition has concrete implications. It means that attempts to regulate platform moderation must account for the expressive nature of these decisions. Governments cannot compel platforms to host or prioritize specific content. Concurrently, the Court's reasoning underscores the quasi-public role of platforms. By analogizing platforms to traditional media, it acknowledges their centrality to public discourse. This creates a tension between private rights and public functions. Platforms are protected as speakers, yet they operate as gatekeepers of the public sphere.

EDITORIAL JUDGMENT IN THE DIGITAL AGE

The concept of editorial judgment has long been associated with newspapers and broadcasters. It refers to the ability to select and organize content in a way that reflects institutional values and priorities. In the digital age, this concept has been extended to platforms. Courts have recognized that the curation of content—whether through human editors or algorithmic systems—constitutes a form of expression.

This raises important questions about the nature of editorial judgment in algorithmic systems. Unlike traditional editors, algorithms operate through predefined rules and data-driven processes. Their outputs may not reflect intentional choices in the same way. The design of these systems involves a series of decisions about what to prioritize, how to rank content, and what to exclude. These decisions are ultimately made by humans, even if they are implemented through automated processes.

Editorial judgment in the digital age is both distributed and mediated. It is exercised through systems rather than individual actors, but it retains its expressive character. This has implications for both law and policy. Recognizing algorithmic curation as protected expression limits the scope of government regulation, while also raising questions about accountability.

DEPLATFORMING AND DEMOCRATIC LEGITIMACY

Deplatforming represents one of the most contested practices in the governance of digital platforms. It involves the suspension or permanent removal of users who violate platform policies, often in cases involving misinformation, incitement, or coordinated harmful behavior. While such actions are typically justified as necessary for maintaining safe and functional environments, they raise threshold questions about legitimacy in a democratic society.

At its core, the debate over deplatforming centers on authority. Platforms are private entities, yet their decisions can have public consequences that rival those of governmental action. When a prominent political figure or movement is removed from a platform, the effects are not limited to that individual or group. They ripple through the broader information ecosystem, shaping what is visible, discussable, and politically salient.

Critics argue that this concentration of power lacks democratic accountability. Platforms are not elected, and their decision-making processes are often opaque. As Suzor (2019) notes, platform governance operates through privately determined rules that may not align with public values or expectations. This creates a legitimacy gap, in which decisions that affect public discourse are made outside traditional democratic channels.

Supporters of deplatforming emphasize the necessity of moderation. Without the ability to remove harmful content, platforms could become dominated by abuse, misinformation, and extremism. Empirical research suggests that deplatforming can reduce the reach of harmful actors, although it may also push them to alternative platforms (Chandrasekharan et al., 2017; Jhaver et al., 2021).

The law surrounding deplatforming reinforces the authority of platforms. In *Manhattan Community Access Corp. v. Halleck* (2019), the Supreme

Court held that private entities operating public access channels were not state actors and therefore not subject to First Amendment constraints. While not directly about social media, the case underscores the principle that private platforms are generally free to regulate speech on their services. Similarly, the *NetChoice* cases reaffirm that platforms' decisions about content moderation are protected forms of expression (*Moody v. NetChoice*, 2024; *NetChoice v. Paxton*, 2024). This means that deplatforming decisions, even when politically consequential, are typically shielded from government interference.

The question, then, is not simply legal but normative. How should societies evaluate the legitimacy of decisions made by private actors that shape public discourse? Some scholars advocate for increased transparency and procedural safeguards, while others call for more robust regulation. Deplatforming highlights a paradox of the digital age: the institutions that structure public discourse are not themselves governed through public processes. Addressing this paradox will require rethinking the relationship between private authority and democratic values.

ARE PLATFORMS PUBLIC FORUMS?

The question of whether digital platforms should be treated as public forums has become one of the most contested issues in contemporary First Amendment law. Public forum doctrine traditionally applies to spaces controlled by the government, such as streets and parks, where speech protections are at their strongest. Extending this doctrine to private platforms would represent a major shift in constitutional interpretation.

Proponents of the public forum analogy argue that platforms function as modern public squares. They provide the primary venues for political communication, civic engagement, and public debate. From this perspective, treating platforms as public forums would ensure that speech rights are protected in the spaces where they matter most.

Courts have consistently resisted this analogy. In *Manhattan Community Access Corp. v. Halleck* (2019), the Supreme Court reaffirmed the principle that private entities are not state actors by virtue of providing forums for speech. The Court emphasized that the First Amendment does not require private parties to host speech they do not wish to host. This distinction has been central to subsequent litigation involving social media platforms. In *NetChoice v. Paxton* (2024), the Court declined to treat platforms as common carriers or public utilities, instead emphasizing their role as expressive entities. This approach aligns with earlier cases recognizing the editorial rights of private actors.

In contextualizing this debate, Napoli and Caplan (2017) argue that platforms' role in shaping information flows complicates traditional distinctions between public and private communication spaces. Meanwhile, Roberts (2019) highlights the labor and institutional structures underlying moderation, suggesting that platforms operate as complex governance systems rather than simple conduits.

Despite these arguments, the law remains anchored in the state action doctrine. Unless platforms are deemed state actors—a threshold that courts have been reluctant to cross—they are not subject to First Amendment constraints in the same way as government entities. This creates a persistent tension. Platforms function as arenas for public discourse, yet they are governed by private rules. Resolving this tension will likely require new conceptual tools that go beyond traditional public forum doctrine.

GOVERNMENT REGULATION AND THE LIMITS OF PLATFORM AUTONOMY

Although digital platforms exercise substantial control over political communication, their autonomy is neither absolute nor unbounded. The laws governing that autonomy are shaped by a combination of constitutional protections, statutory provisions, and evolving judicial interpretation. Efforts to regulate digital platforms have intensified in recent years, reflecting growing concern about their influence over political communication. These efforts have taken various forms, including laws targeting content moderation, competition, and data practices. However, they face real legal and practical constraints.

Central to this approach is the recognition that platform moderation constitutes a form of protected expression. As established earlier, the Supreme Court's approach in the *NetChoice* cases treated platform moderation as a form of expressive conduct, placing it within the core protections of the First Amendment. By affirming that platforms exercise editorial judgment in digital environments, the Court ensured that state efforts to compel or prohibit specific viewpoint moderation are subject to strict constitutional scrutiny.

The implication is clear: platforms cannot be easily transformed into neutral conduits without infringing on their expressive rights, and governments cannot compel platforms to host or prioritize specific content.

This places hard constraints on regulatory strategies that seek to directly control platform behavior. However, the Court did not suggest that platforms are beyond regulation altogether, leaving open the possibility of narrower forms of regulation. Instead, it signaled that certain forms of regulation—particularly those that do not directly interfere with editorial discretion—may be permissible. This includes requirements related to transparency, reporting, and procedural fairness, which aim to enhance accountability without dictating substantive outcomes. Similarly, antitrust enforcement and data protection laws operate through different legal channels that may avoid First Amendment concerns.

This distinction reflects a broader tension in platform governance. On one hand, platforms are private entities entitled to constitutional protection. On the other hand, they perform functions that are central to democratic life. As Balkin (2018) argues, platforms occupy a hybrid role as "information fiduciaries," suggesting that their responsibilities may extend beyond those of ordinary private actors. Illuminating the obstacles to effective regulation, Gillespie (2018) demonstrates that moderation systems are deeply entangled with platform design and governance, making them difficult to disentangle from broader questions of institutional authority. Similarly, Kaye (2019) emphasizes that international human rights policies may provide a more flexible alternative basis for evaluating platform responsibilities, particularly in global contexts.

The result is a legal environment characterized by partial autonomy. Platforms retain substantial control over their operations, but that control exists within a web of constitutional constraints and growing regulatory attention. The regulatory landscape is further complicated by the global nature of platforms. Policies adopted in one jurisdiction can have effects in others, creating conflicts between legal regimes. The limits of government regulation reflect both constitutional constraints and the inherent characteristics of platforms themselves. Any effective approach must navigate these tensions while balancing competing values. Understanding this balance is essential for analyzing the future of platform governance.

THE PLATFORM-STATE RELATIONSHIP

The relationship between platforms and the state is complex and interdependent. Platforms are not merely subjects of regulation; they are also partners, intermediaries, and sometimes competitors in the exercise of governance.

Governments rely on platforms to disseminate information, particularly during crises. Public health campaigns, emergency alerts, and election-related messaging are often distributed through social media. At the same time, platforms cooperate with law enforcement, providing data and assistance in investigations. This collaboration raises questions about the boundaries between public and private authority. When platforms act in coordination with government, they may take on quasi-public roles. Courts have generally maintained the distinction between state action and private conduct.

The platform-state relationship is also shaped by influence. Platforms participate in policy debates, lobby regulators, and shape the development of laws. Their economic and social significance gives them substantial leverage in these interactions.

Scholars such as Napoli and Caplan (2017) emphasize the need to understand this relationship as a form of co-governance, arguing that platforms and governments jointly shape the information environment, even when their interests diverge. This hybrid model destabilizes traditional conceptions of sovereignty and authority. It suggests that governance in the digital age is distributed across multiple actors and institutions.

POWER WITHOUT OFFICE

Platforms do not hold public office, yet they exercise power that is unmistakably political. They shape agendas, regulate speech, and influence participation in ways that rival traditional institutions. This power is distinctive in several respects. It is private rather than public, distributed rather than centralized, and housed in systems rather than exercised through individual decisions. These characteristics make it both pervasive and difficult to regulate.

The analysis in this chapter suggests that platforms should be understood as political institutions, even though they do not fit neatly within existing categories. They perform governance functions that affect democratic life, yet they operate outside traditional mechanisms of accountability. This raises urgent questions about the future of democracy. How can societies ensure that platforms act in ways that are consistent with public values? What forms of oversight are appropriate for institutions that are both private and public in their effects?

This dynamic illustrates the necessity of infrastructural constitutionalism. When we analyze platform moderation strictly through the lens of traditional

First Amendment jurisprudence—asking whether the state has impermissibly coerced a private actor—we miss the architectural reality of the platform itself. To protect democratic discourse, First Amendment values must be deliberately embedded into the platform's underlying design—its sorting algorithms, engagement metrics, and amplification pathways—rather than relying solely on ex post legal mandates or user terms of service. The code itself must become the constitutional safeguard.

Since digital platforms exercise quasi-regulatory power over public discourse while sheltering behind First Amendment protections that foreclose direct content regulation, the governance response must target structure rather than speech. Platforms must provide meaningful transparency into the ranking and curation systems that determine political visibility—not source-code disclosure, but functional accountability for the amplification architectures that shape what citizens see. Regulations should target the speed and mechanics of viral amplification and behavioral data harvesting rather than the substance of any particular message, preserving editorial freedom while constraining the foundational design choices that distort democratic communication. And platforms should be treated as information fiduciaries with formal duties of care regarding how they harvest and deploy user data—obligations that flow from their infrastructural role in democratic life rather than from any determination of content liability (Balkin, 2018). The full regulatory architecture for platform accountability is developed in the final chapter.

3

INVISIBLE POWER AND ELECTIONS: DATA, TARGETING, AND THE NEW CAMPAIGN MACHINE

Unlike the established administrative mechanisms examined in other chapters, electoral data and algorithmic microtargeting exist within a persistent regulatory vacuum. In the United States, electoral data regulation remains one of the least-developed domains of algorithmic governance. Consequently, this chapter is necessarily more diagnostic than prescriptive. By leaning on established political science literature to map the invisible power dynamics of modern elections, we can better understand exactly why current constitutional and administrative law is struggling to keep pace with these technologies.

Hybrid governance's reliance on data infrastructures reshapes the democratic process itself, transforming elections from shared public events into fragmented, microtargeted information systems. For most of the 20th century, electoral politics functioned as a system of mass communication. Contemporary elections operate through systems of data-driven precision influence in which campaigns address highly specific audience segments, often at the level of the individual voter. Rather than communicating through a shared public sphere, campaigns now deliver differentiated messages across fragmented digital environments (Bennett & Lyon, 2019).

The shift is not merely technological but epistemic. Campaigns no longer rely primarily on intuition, ideological positioning, or traditional polling. Instead, they draw upon large-scale data infrastructures that enable probabilistic assessments of voter behavior. Voters are evaluated not only in terms of their demographic characteristics but also through behavioral, psychological, and consumption patterns derived from digital traces (Kreiss, 2016).

This institutional reconfiguration has implications for democratic practice. In a broadcast model, campaign messages were publicly visible and subject to scrutiny by opponents, journalists, and voters themselves. In contrast, data-driven campaigning operates through largely opaque channels in which different voters receive different messages, often without awareness of the broader communication environment (Tufekci, 2014). As a result, elections resemble complex information systems rather than public deliberative processes. Understanding this systemic change requires examining the mechanisms that underpin it: microtargeting, behavioral nudging, voter segmentation, and the emergence of campaigns as data-intensive operations.

MICROTARGETING AND THE ARCHITECTURE OF INFLUENCE

Microtargeting refers to the practice of tailoring political messages to narrowly defined segments of the electorate based on detailed data profiles. While earlier forms of targeted communication existed—particularly in direct mail campaigns—the scale and sophistication of contemporary microtargeting are unprecedented. At its foundation, microtargeting involves three interrelated processes: data aggregation, predictive modeling, and targeted delivery.

Data aggregation draws upon multiple sources. Voter registration files provide baseline political information, including turnout history and party affiliation. These are supplemented by commercial datasets that capture consumer behavior, income estimates, and lifestyle indicators. Digital platforms contribute behavioral data such as browsing activity, social media engagement, and location tracking. Together, these datasets enable the construction of highly granular voter profiles (Bennett & Lyon, 2019).

Predictive modeling translates these data into actionable insights. Campaigns employ statistical techniques to generate scores indicating a voter's likelihood of supporting a candidate, turning out to vote, or responding to specific messages. These models do not predict behavior with certainty but provide probabilistic guidance for strategic decision-making (Kreiss, 2016).

Targeted delivery occurs through digital platforms that allow campaigns to disseminate customized messages to specific audiences. Social media advertising systems enable campaigns to define target audiences based on detailed criteria, including interests, behaviors, and inferred attributes. This capacity allows for the simultaneous deployment of thousands of message variants tailored to different voter segments (Tufekci, 2014). The implications of this architecture are far-reaching. Microtargeting enables campaigns to move beyond generalized appeals and instead engage voters through highly personalized messaging. But this personalization comes at the cost of transparency. Because targeted messages are not publicly broadcast, they are difficult to monitor and regulate. Empirical research suggests that microtargeting can influence voter behavior, particularly in close elections where marginal shifts in turnout or persuasion can alter outcomes (Hersh, 2015). Scholars caution that its effects are often overstated and contingent upon context, message quality, and voter predispositions. Nevertheless, the underlying shift remains clear: political communication has moved from a public, shared domain to a fragmented system of individualized interactions.

BEHAVIORAL NUDGING AND THE PSYCHOLOGY OF VOTING

Microtargeting is frequently combined with behavioral nudging, a set of techniques derived from behavioral economics that aim to influence decision-making through subtle interventions rather than explicit persuasion. The concept of nudging is grounded in the work of Thaler and Sunstein (2008), who argue that small changes in the "choice architecture" can significantly affect behavior. In the electoral context, nudges are used to increase turnout, shape perceptions, and influence political preferences.

One widely studied mechanism is *social norm messaging*. Individuals are more likely to engage in behaviors they perceive as common or expected within their social group. Field experiments have demonstrated that informing voters about the voting behavior of their neighbors can increase turnout, sometimes substantially (Gerber et al., 2008).

Another mechanism involves *emotional framing*. Political messages that evoke strong emotions—such as fear or enthusiasm—are more likely to capture attention and motivate action. Digital targeting allows campaigns to align emotional appeals with the specific concerns of different voter segments, enhancing their effectiveness (Tufekci, 2014).

A more subtle form of influence is *timing and placement optimization*. Digital platforms enable campaigns to deliver messages at moments when individuals are most likely to be receptive, based on patterns of online activity. This temporal precision increases the likelihood that messages will be noticed and acted upon.

Importantly, behavioral nudging often operates below the level of conscious awareness. Unlike traditional persuasion, which relies on argumentation and evidence, nudging leverages cognitive biases and heuristics. This raises normative questions about autonomy and informed consent. If voters are influenced through mechanisms they do not fully perceive, the legitimacy of their choices may be called into question. The integration of nudging with microtargeting intensifies these concerns. By tailoring nudges to individual psychological profiles, campaigns can maximize their effectiveness while minimizing visibility. This combination marks a sharp departure from traditional models of democratic persuasion.

DATA FIRMS AND THE INDUSTRIALIZATION OF VOTER SEGMENTATION

The rise of data-driven campaigning has been accompanied by the emergence of specialized data firms that provide analytics, modeling, and targeting services to political campaigns. These firms play a major role in transforming raw data into strategic insights, effectively industrializing voter segmentation.

Data firms aggregate information from diverse sources to construct detailed voter profiles. They then apply segmentation techniques to divide the electorate into categories based on shared characteristics. These categories may be demographic, behavioral, or psychographic. Psychographic segmentation, which seeks to infer personality traits and values from behavioral data, has received particular attention following high-profile controversies involving firms such as Cambridge Analytica. While the effectiveness of such techniques remains debated, their use reflects a broader trend toward granular forms of voter analysis (Isaak & Hanna, 2018).

Beyond segmentation, data firms often provide comprehensive services, including message testing, digital advertising, and performance analytics. Campaigns may rely heavily on these firms, effectively outsourcing key aspects of their operations. This outsourcing raises questions about accountability. Decisions about targeting and messaging may be made by private entities that are not directly accountable to voters. Moreover, the proprietary nature of data models and algorithms limits transparency, making it difficult to assess their accuracy or fairness.

The involvement of data firms also introduces new risks related to data security and privacy. The aggregation of sensitive information creates potential vulnerabilities, as demonstrated by incidents involving data breaches and misuse of personal information (Isaak & Hanna, 2018). From a regulatory perspective, data firms occupy a complex position. They are not traditional political actors, yet their activities reshape electoral processes in ways existing law was not designed to govern. Existing legal frameworks may not adequately address their role, creating gaps in oversight.

CAMPAIGNS AS DATA OPERATIONS

One of the most consequential developments in modern elections is the transformation of campaigns into data-driven operations. While messaging remains important, it is often nested within a broader system of data collection, analysis, and optimization.

Contemporary campaigns are organized around data infrastructures. Dedicated teams of analysts, data scientists, and digital strategists play a key role in decision-making. Campaign strategies are informed by continuous streams of data, enabling real-time adjustments to targeting and messaging (Kreiss, 2016).

A key feature of this approach is the use of *feedback loops*. Digital platforms provide immediate information about how users interact with campaign content—clicks, shares, comments, and conversions. These data are used to refine targeting models and optimize message delivery.

Campaigns also employ *A/B testing*, a technique borrowed from commercial marketing, in which different versions of a message are tested on subsets of an audience to determine which performs best. Successful variants are then scaled up, while less effective ones are discarded. This iterative process transforms campaigning into a form of continuous experimentation. Rather than relying on fixed strategies, campaigns adapt dynamically to changing conditions and new information.

The data-driven nature of campaigns also affects resource allocation. By identifying high-value targets—such as persuadable voters in competitive districts—campaigns can focus their efforts more efficiently. However, this targeted approach may lead to unequal attention across different segments of the electorate, potentially reinforcing existing disparities in political engagement (Hersh, 2015).

FRAGMENTATION OF THE PUBLIC SPHERE

The rise of personalized political communication has contributed to the fragmentation of the public sphere. In the broadcast era, voters were exposed to a relatively shared set of information through mass media. This common informational environment facilitated public debate and collective deliberation.

In contrast, microtargeting and personalized messaging create divergent informational experiences. Different voters receive different messages, tailored to their data profiles. As a result, the electorate may no longer share a common understanding of political issues (Bennett & Lyon, 2019). This fragmentation has several implications. First, it complicates public deliberation, as individuals may base their opinions on different sets of information. Second, it undermines accountability, as candidates can present inconsistent messages to different audiences without being easily detected. Third, it may contribute to polarization by reinforcing existing preferences and biases.

Digital platforms play a key role in this process. Their algorithms prioritize content that generates engagement, often amplifying emotionally charged or polarizing material. Campaigns operate within this environment, leveraging platform dynamics to maximize the reach and impact of their messages (Tufekci, 2014).

LEGAL AND REGULATORY DEFICITS

The transformation of electoral campaigning strains laws and regulations that were designed for an earlier era. Existing election laws were developed in an era of mass communication and may not adequately address the complexities of data-driven campaigning.

One area of concern is *transparency*. Regulations governing political advertising often focus on disclosure requirements, but these may not capture the full scope of microtargeted messaging. Because targeted ads are not publicly visible, they can evade traditional forms of oversight.

Legal debates surrounding digital political communication have begun to reach courts. Directly relevant are emerging cases involving platform regulation. As explored earlier, rulings like *Moody v. NetChoice* (2024) define the extent to which states can constitutionally regulate these digital moderation practices. These cases pose direct questions about the balance between free expression and regulatory authority in digital environments.

Privacy is another critical issue. The use of personal data for political purposes raises questions about consent and surveillance. While data protection laws such as the General Data Protection Regulation (GDPR) in the European Union (EU) provide some safeguards, comparable laws in other jurisdictions remain fragmented. The regulatory landscape is further complicated by the role of private actors, including data firms and digital platforms. These entities exercise outsized influence over electoral processes but are not always subject to the same obligations as traditional political actors.

DEMOCRATIC LEGITIMACY AND ELECTORAL INTEGRITY

The rise of data-driven campaigning raises core questions about democratic legitimacy. Elections are not only mechanisms for selecting leaders but also processes through which citizens engage with political ideas and make collective decisions. If voter behavior is shaped by personalized, data-driven influence, the nature of democratic participation may change.

On one hand, targeted communication can enhance engagement by making political messages more relevant to individual concerns. On the other hand, it may undermine deliberation by replacing public debate with private persuasion. Scholars have debated whether microtargeting strengthens or weakens democracy. Some argue that it increases efficiency and responsiveness, enabling campaigns to connect with voters more effectively. Others contend that it creates opportunities for manipulation and reduces transparency (Bennett & Lyon, 2019). The question of legitimacy depends on how these technologies are used and governed. Ensuring that data-driven campaigning aligns with democratic principles requires careful consideration of transparency, accountability, and fairness.

ELECTIONS WITHOUT A SHARED STAGE

Modern elections take place in fragmented, data-driven environments where campaigns operate as sophisticated information systems. Microtargeting, behavioral nudging, and voter segmentation have transformed the nature of political communication, shifting it from a public, shared process to a series of individualized interactions. This reconfiguration does not eliminate traditional forms of campaigning but reconfigures their role within a broader ecosystem of data-driven influence. Elections are no longer conducted solely through speeches, debates, and advertisements; they are also shaped by algorithms, data models, and digital platforms.

The implications for democracy are profound. The fragmentation of the public sphere, the opacity of targeted messaging, and the concentration of power in data infrastructures all erode traditional notions of transparency and accountability. As data-driven infrastructures fragment the electoral public sphere, they concurrently destabilize the legal architecture of the American administrative state. What has not kept pace is the law: the electoral arena remains the least regulated domain of the algorithmic state, a persistent vacuum in which the most consequential decisions about democratic participation are made through invisible, ungoverned systems.

The systemic vulnerabilities identified by Kreiss, Tufekci, and Bennett and Lyon have only compounded in the 2024 election cycle, bringing the limitations of current administrative oversight into sharp relief—most notably in the largely unregulated data broker market and the Federal Election Commission's (FEC's) fraught attempts to govern artificial intelligence (AI)-generated advertising.

THE LIMITS OF CURRENT OVERSIGHT: DATA BROKERS AND THE FEC

While the preceding analysis makes clear that algorithmic microtargeting has altered the political landscape, the resulting regulatory crisis has not been met with a symmetrical legal response. Instead, the current legal and regulatory environment is sparse, fragmented, and ill-equipped to address the complexities of modern, data-driven campaigning.

To understand this failure of oversight, we must examine two critical domains where a combination of regulatory gaps and institutional limitations creates a persistent vacuum: the largely unregulated market for political data and the FEC's ongoing struggle to assert its authority over AI-generated advertising.

THE DATA BROKER LOOPHOLE

The foundational engine of modern political microtargeting is the commercial data broker industry. These companies compile, aggregate, and resell vast quantities of personal information from disparate sources, enabling political campaigns to build extraordinarily detailed psychological profiles of individual voters. However, these activities operate within a glaring regulatory loophole. While sectoral privacy laws exist in the United States, they are largely irrelevant in this context. Political data brokers are not subject to the Health Insurance Portability and Accountability Act (HIPAA), as they are not covered health entities. Similarly, the detailed dossiers they compile for targeting purposes—containing sensitive information on finances, demographics, and consumer behavior—do not constitute "consumer reports" under the Fair Credit Reporting Act (FCRA), because they are not being used for credit, employment, or insurance decisions. This absence of a comprehensive federal privacy statute allows a vast, largely invisible data-gathering ecosystem to feed the targeting operations of political actors without any real accountability.

Furthermore, any attempt to regulate this data ecosystem—and by extension, the targeting that relies on it—is immediately complicated by the First Amendment. The Supreme Court has long afforded political speech the highest level of constitutional protection. Consequently, legal arguments about voter privacy or the harmful effects of microtargeting frequently collide with established precedents that view campaign activity as a core democratic expression. These First Amendment constraints make it difficult to craft regulations that address the *method* of speech (data-driven targeting) without being seen as an impermissible restriction on the *content* of political speech itself. The resulting legal environment is one where the data broker loophole remains open, protected by a potent combination of sectoral regulatory failure and robust constitutional defenses of campaign activity.

Viewed through the lens of infrastructural constitutionalism, the commercial data broker ecosystem is not merely a privacy vulnerability; it is a foundational architecture that dictates democratic participation. If we accept that electoral data architecture is the modern infrastructure of voting and campaigning, then leaving it entirely to private market optimization undermines democratic equality. Infrastructural constitutionalism demands that we regulate these data pipelines not just as commercial assets, but as critical democratic utilities.

THE FEC'S JURISDICTIONAL STRUGGLE

The regulatory vacuum is perhaps most evident in the FEC's approach to algorithmic and AI-driven advertising, which became a dominant concern during the 2024 election cycle. The proliferation of cheap, sophisticated generative AI tools led to a wave of deepfakes and manipulated media, dramatically escalating the threat to an informed electorate. The FEC, however, has struggled to respond effectively, exposing a deep tension in administrative law. While the commission has engaged in recent and ongoing rulemaking to address AI-generated ads, its actions are severely constrained by the scope of its statutory authority. The FEC's primary mandate regarding misleading information is limited to prohibiting "fraudulent misrepresentation" by one candidate or campaign about another.

This narrow authority cannot address the modern AI threat. It cannot, for example, easily address AI-generated disinformation about the election process itself (such as fake robocalls providing incorrect polling locations), nor can it regulate AI ads that do not specifically impersonate a competing campaign but are instead generic or issue-based deceptions. Attempts to broadly regulate AI ads to prevent general voter confusion or protect democratic integrity would almost certainly run afoul of the constitutional limits discussed above or exceed the agency's clear congressional mandate. As a result, the FEC is caught in a jurisdictional trap, unable to devise a comprehensive regulatory solution even as technological capabilities accelerate, leaving the domain of algorithmic governance law in elections largely undefined.

Because campaigns now operate as opaque data systems that bypass the shared informational environment on which democratic deliberation depends, electoral regulation must reach the mechanisms through which political influence is actually exercised. Campaign finance and advertising disclosure laws should be extended to capture the granular, personalized nature of digital microtargeting—voters are entitled to know not only that they are being addressed, but through what data and on what basis. Consent requirements are needed for the extraction and political use of psychographic and behavioral data, treating electoral profiling as a practice requiring affirmative public authorization rather than a commercial activity governed only by terms of service. And private data brokers and political analytics firms—the unseen infrastructure of modern campaigns—must be brought within the perimeter of electoral regulatory oversight. The current regulatory vacuum in this domain is the subject of the final chapter's most urgent legislative proposals.

4

LAW AND THE ALGORITHMIC STATE: DUE PROCESS, OPAQUE SYSTEMS, AND REGULATORY LAG

Just as opaque data infrastructures have transformed the political sphere by turning elections into fragmented, microtargeted information systems, these same technologies are now destabilizing the legal architecture of the American administrative state.

The Supreme Court's decision in *Loper Bright* (2024) fundamentally altered the administrative-law landscape by overruling *Chevron* (1984) and rejecting mandatory judicial deference—generating precisely the paradox identified in the introduction. This chapter examines how that paradox is now playing out within administrative law, agency practice, and the federal courts.

THE COMPUTATIONAL TURN IN THE ADMINISTRATIVE STATE

Artificial intelligence (AI) does not displace the administrative state; it alters how it operates. As comprehensive audits reveal, many federal agencies have already integrated thousands of predictive systems, biometric matching tools, and automated workflows into their daily operations, governed by an expanding web of statutes and executive guidance (US Government Accountability Office [GAO], 2023, 2025). These computational systems do not eliminate human decision-making, but they reconfigure it, shifting the locus of influence away from the final, visible act of decision toward earlier stages of ranking, flagging, and inference. The legal issue is therefore not whether agencies may adopt more sophisticated tools; they already have.

The deeper question is whether constitutional due process and ordinary administrative law can still discipline government action when this inherent opacity frustrates the Administrative Procedure Act's (APA's) demand for reasoned decision-making and reviewable records.

It is essential to distinguish the three generations of computational governance this shift encompasses, as they pose constitutionally distinct problems. First-generation rule-based expert systems encode explicit human-authored logic; their opacity is manageable because their rules can in principle be audited. Second-generation statistical machine-learning systems—the primary subject of this book's case studies, including COMPAS, Management Information and Data Analytics Strategy (MiDAS), and Medicaid eligibility platforms—infer patterns from historical data; their opacity is inherent because their internal representations resist human interpretation. Third-generation generative AI and large language models introduce a qualitatively different problem: they produce naturalistic, seemingly reasoned outputs that can simulate the kind of explanation administrative law requires, without actually providing it (Bender et al., 2021; Bommasani et al., 2021; Weidinger et al., 2021). A government agency that deploys a large language model to draft denial letters has not satisfied the *Mathews v. Eldridge* (1976) requirement of meaningful contestability merely because the output reads fluently. The appearance of reason is not the substance of reason, and the post-Loper Bright judiciary must be alert to that distinction.

ADMINISTRATIVE LAW BEFORE AI: REASONED DECISION-MAKING

Administrative law has long required agencies to act within their statutory authority and to provide reasons adequate for review. In *SEC v. Chenery Corp.* (1943), the Supreme Court held that agency action must stand or fall on the rationale the agency itself gave. *Citizens to Preserve Overton Park, Inc. v. Volpe* (1971) reinforced the duty of courts to conduct meaningful review, while *Motor Vehicle Manufacturers Association v. State Farm Mutual Automobile Insurance Co.* (1983) made clear that arbitrary-and-capricious review requires agencies to consider relevant factors and explain their decisions with care.

Those principles are of particular importance in an AI context because machine-assisted decisions tempt agencies to compress explanation into assertion. Once a system produces a score, risk level, anomaly flag, or confidence assessment, institutional actors may treat the output as self-validating because it appears technical. But administrative law does not recognize "the model said so" as a sufficient reason. If an AI output shapes a legal consequence, the agency must still be able to explain why the output is relevant and why reliance on it is consistent with the governing statute.

CHEVRON'S LIMITS AND THE IMPACT OF LOPER BRIGHT (2024)

For decades, *Chevron* deference appeared to offer a mechanism for adapting law to changing conditions, as courts deferred to reasonable agency interpretations of ambiguous statutes (1984). Yet *Chevron*'s apparent adaptability masked deeper limitations. It was a doctrine about statutory interpretation, not about the legitimacy or opacity of decision-making processes. By encouraging courts to defer to agency expertise, it allowed agencies to adopt new methods of governance without always confronting the full implications for transparency and accountability.

As this paradox makes plain, agencies must now defend their actions on the merits without the shield of broad deference, yet those actions are shaped by computational systems that inherently resist straightforward explanation. This demand for clearer reasons is compounded by recent Supreme Court decisions like *Department of Commerce v. New York* (2019) and *Department of Homeland Security v. Regents of the University of California* (2020), which insist that agencies must provide real, reviewable reasons rather than thin or pretextual ones. In a post-*Chevron* environment, opacity becomes even harder to defend.

This paradox is playing out in the federal courts, where Loper Bright (2024) is being aggressively utilized to dismantle agency rulemakings. In *Chamber of Commerce of the United States of America v. Environmental Protection Agency* (2024), the court's rigorous, unforgiving scrutiny of the agency's statutory authority illustrates the broader pattern now cascading through the lower courts: if an older law does not explicitly mention algorithms or automated systems, courts applying post-Loper Bright textualism are increasingly concluding that agencies lack authority to regulate them—a doctrinal pattern still in early appellate flux, and not yet settled by the Supreme Court.

It is crucial to recognize that these district and circuit court interpretations represent the initial judicial tremors of *Loper Bright* (2024), not the final doctrinal settlement. Until the Supreme Court explicitly reviews and binds the boundaries of these lower court applications, agency authority over algorithmic tools remains in a state of active appellate flux. Lower courts are currently navigating what this book terms *Shadow Skidmore* deference—a doctrinally unstable environment, analogous to the pre-*Chevron* persuasiveness standard articulated in *Skidmore v. Swift & Co.* (1944), where judges now weigh agency expertise only to the extent they find it independently persuasive, without the mandatory deference *Chevron* once supplied.

This shift reflects a broader transformation toward infrastructural constitutionalism, the embedding of constitutional principles within technical architecture—which this book has argued is the necessary governance response to this hybrid state.

This demand for explicit justification is compounded by the immediate downstream effects of *Loper Bright* (2024). Federal courts have aggressively leveraged this precedent to destabilize early attempts at algorithmic governance. Agencies like the Federal Trade Commission (FTC), which have historically relied on broad statutory mandates prohibiting "unfair methods of competition" to police data harvesting and algorithmic bias, now find their rulemakings highly vulnerable to judicial invalidation without highly specific congressional authorization. This vulnerability was further magnified by the Court's 2024 decision in *Corner Post.* By ruling that the statute of limitations for challenging an agency action under the APA begins when a plaintiff is harmed—rather than when the rule was finalized—*Corner Post* acts as a potent multiplier for *Loper Bright* (2024). It allows industry actors to challenge foundational data, environmental, and privacy regulations that predate the current computational boom, threatening to unravel established administrative guardrails just as the algorithmic state demands more robust oversight.

OPAQUE POWER ACROSS FEDERAL DOMAINS

The law's struggle to catch up becomes particularly acute in high-stakes domains where the consequences of administrative action involve liberty, security, or subsistence. Across the federal government, automated systems are quietly collapsing the distinction between administrative support and final decision-making. In homeland security and immigration, for instance, biometric identification and predictive screening can alter the trajectory of a case long before a formal adjudication occurs, demonstrating that the true due-process danger often lies in the hidden steering power of intermediate classification (Department of Homeland Security [DHS], 2024; GAO, 2024).

Similarly, in the criminal justice system, seemingly advisory risk-assessment tools—such as the Bureau of Prisons' PATTERN system—meaningfully dictate program eligibility and prerelease pathways, raising the exact transparency concerns the Wisconsin Supreme Court warned of in *State v. Loomis* (2016) (Federal Bureau of Prisons, 2026). This opaque mediation extends even to foundational property interests like healthcare benefits; when agencies test machine learning to expedite prior authorizations, algorithmic flags introduce delay and friction that can effectively deny medically necessary care (CMS, 2025).

THE FTC AND THE EMERGENCE OF PROACTIVE ALGORITHMIC OVERSIGHT

While the post-*Loper Bright* environment has narrowed the legal ground on which agencies may operate, the FTC has pursued a parallel strategy: using its existing Section 5 authority to establish, through enforcement rather than rulemaking, a body of norms governing algorithmic design and deployment. Two developments between 2023 and 2024 mark a decisive shift in the FTC's approach—from litigating individual harms to constructing anticipatory accountability requirements for AI systems prior to deployment.

The first is the FTC's December 2023 complaint against Rite Aid Corporation. The action is doctrinally significant because, for the first time, the FTC invoked Section 5 of the FTC Act (15 U.S.C. § 45) on grounds of algorithmic bias specifically, challenging Rite Aid's deployment of facial recognition surveillance technology in its retail stores without adequate bias testing or safeguards against false positives (Federal Trade Commission [FTC], 2023a). The FTC alleged that the technology disproportionately misidentified Black, Asian, Latino, and women consumers as matching criminal watch list entries, leading to public accusations, detentions, and police calls based on faulty algorithmic outputs (FTC, 2023a). The proposed consent order required Rite Aid not only to cease use of facial recognition technology for five years, but also to delete all biometric data, models, and algorithms derived from that data—a remedy now referred to in enforcement practice as "algorithmic disgorgement" (FTC, 2023b). In his statement on the action, FTC Commissioner Alvaro Bedoya made the regulatory intention explicit, describing the consent order as a baseline for what a comprehensive algorithmic fairness program should look like and signaling that future violators should expect appointment of an independent assessor. The Rite Aid action is constitutionally significant not simply as an enforcement outcome but as a doctrinal signal: biased algorithmic design is itself an unfair practice under Section 5, independent of any specific showing of discriminatory intent.

The second development is the September 2024 launch of Operation AI Comply, through which the FTC announced five simultaneous enforcement actions against companies deploying or marketing AI systems in deceptive or unfair ways (FTC, 2024). The initiative's significance lies less in the individual cases than in the institutional form they represent. By codifying a named enforcement sweep—rather than proceeding case by case—the FTC signaled a transition from reactive adjudication of specific harms to proactive oversight of AI deployment practices (FTC, 2024). As Chair Lina Khan stated in announcing the initiative: "Using AI tools to trick, mislead, or defraud people is illegal. There is no AI exemption from the laws on the books" (FTC, 2024).

Together, these developments constitute an emergent federal enforcement strategy that operates below the threshold of formal rulemaking and therefore below the level at which *Loper Bright* most acutely bites. They represent the FTC attempting precisely what this book's theory of infrastructural constitutionalism recommends: building accountability requirements—bias testing, auditability, data minimization, and explainability—into the design and marketing of AI systems before those systems cause harm, rather than litigating the consequences. The deeper question, addressed in the sections that follow, is whether enforcement alone can substitute for the systematic regulatory architecture that rulemaking would provide—and whether the FTC's statutory authority, now under heightened judicial scrutiny, is sufficient to sustain the oversight role it is attempting to assume.

THE EVIDENTIARY FRONTIER AND REGULATORY LAG

The law's struggle to adapt is also highly visible in the domain of evidence. In 2025 and 2026, Judicial Conference of the United States reported ongoing consideration of a proposed new Federal Rule of Evidence 707 addressing machine-generated evidence (Judicial Conference of the United States, 2025; 2026). Because proposed federal rules must navigate a multi-year process of public comment, Supreme Court approval, and a congressional review period before taking effect, FRE 707 currently serves as an indicator of systemic judicial concern rather than an enforceable evidentiary standard. This highlights a deeper conceptual fault line: if a machine's output cannot be meaningfully explained or challenged, it raises questions about whether it can be integrated into an adversarial system without undermining its foundations.

Beyond the courts, the executive branch has developed evolving governance initiatives. Notably, the initial policy established by Memorandum M-24-10 (Office of Management and Budget [OMB], 2024) was rescinded in April 2025 and replaced by Memorandum M-25-21 (OMB, 2025), reflecting a policy shift toward accelerating AI adoption and innovation. These efforts are further supplemented by technical guidelines like the AI Risk Management Framework (National Institute of Standards and Technology [NIST], 2023).

TOWARD DUE-PROCESS STANDARDS FOR COMPUTATIONAL ADMINISTRATION

This doctrinal paradox leaves both agencies and affected citizens in a precarious position: courts now demand explicit, legible statutory reasoning, yet the computational tools driving administrative action resist such explanation. Resolving this paradox requires more than just retreating from algorithmic tools; it requires establishing a new procedural baseline. If agencies can no longer rely on broad judicial deference to shield their opaque systems, they must proactively build transparency and contestability into the systems themselves. The constitutional response to administrative AI, therefore, does not require a wholly new legal doctrine; rather, existing due process principles must be translated into computational realities. The operative constitutional standard remains the tripartite balancing test established in *Mathews v. Eldridge* (1976): courts weigh the private interest affected, the risk of erroneous deprivation through existing procedures and the probable value of additional safeguards, and the government's interest in administrative efficiency. Each of these factors is systematically distorted by algorithmic opacity—the private interest is unchanged or heightened, the risk of erroneous deprivation increases as procedures become less legible, and the government's efficiency interest is routinely overstated as a justification for foreclosing contestability. To survive strict judicial scrutiny in a post-*Chevron* landscape, agencies must adopt a procedural baseline anchored in the following requirements:

- *Material Influence:* Courts and agencies should ask whether a tool materially influenced the pathway to an adverse or burdening result, not only whether it made the final determination.
- *Specific Notice:* Affected persons should be told when automated processing materially shaped their case, what category of judgment it influenced, and what core factual issues drove the result.
- *Meaningful Contestability:* Agencies should provide access to the data, categories, and inferences that mattered in the individual case, combined with a route to contest them before deprivation where feasible.
- *Reviewable Records:* Agencies should preserve an administratively reviewable record of model use to allow for meaningful APA review.
- *Heightened Caution:* Liberty- and subsistence-affecting settings must presumptively require stronger explanation and contestability than low-stakes internal optimization tools.
- *Candid Uncertainty:* Agencies must be candid about probabilistic uncertainty and explain what the model does and does not show.

The primary danger is not simply that computers will replace human officials, but that agencies will continue to speak the language of human judgment while practical power quietly migrates into systems that affected persons cannot see, understand, or dispute. The future of lawful AI in the administrative state therefore depends on a simple but demanding principle: computational governance must remain government by reasons.

Because agencies can no longer rely on judicial deference to shield opaque computational systems from intensive legal scrutiny, they must proactively build transparency and contestability into those systems rather than asserting it subsequently. Citizens must be informed when an automated process materially shapes an adverse outcome— notice cannot be limited to the final determination when the determinative influence occurred earlier in the pipeline. Agencies must provide human-readable explanations of the variables and inferences that drove an algorithmic result, together with a clear and accessible pathway for appeal before deprivation where feasible. And to survive the post-*Loper Bright* demand for reviewable statutory reasoning, agencies must preserve the operational logic of their models in a form adequate for meaningful APA review. These requirements translate the *Mathews v. Eldridge* (1976) balancing test into computational realities; their statutory codification is developed in the D-APA proposal of the final chapter.

5

INEQUALITY IN THE ALGORITHMIC STATE

The opaque systems driving this hybrid state do not merely automate administration; they operationalize and reorganize systemic inequality through code, data, and predictive modeling. What makes this realignment unique is the phenomenon of *digital redlining*, where exclusion becomes personalized, probabilistic, and remarkably difficult to prove. While automated systems are sold on the promise of objective efficiency, they function as a *recursive state*—feeding on the outputs of earlier biased institutions to generate new data that hardens historical hierarchies into the operating logic of governance itself (Barocas & Selbst, 2016; Selbst et al., 2019; Suresh & Guttag, 2021).

From this perspective, inequality in the algorithmic state is not merely a failure of implementation but a failure of infrastructural constitutionalism, where constitutional commitments to equal protection are not adequately translated into system design.

At stake is more than flawed software; the main problem is institutional. Automated systems are introduced into domains already marked by racial inequality, class stratification, geographic segregation, and unequal access to political voice. In such settings, data is not a neutral mirror of social reality. It is a residue of previous decisions, unequal opportunities, and asymmetric surveillance. When those conditions are ignored, the algorithmic state does not simply inherit social inequality; it operationalizes it. The result is a mode of governance in which old exclusions are translated into new computational forms, often with less visibility and fewer opportunities for contestation than in the traditional administrative state (Citron & Pasquale, 2014; National Institute of Standards and Technology [NIST], 2023; Office of Science and Technology Policy [OSTP], 2022).

BIAS IN DATASETS AND THE FICTION OF NEUTRAL INPUT

Much public discussion of artificial intelligence (AI) assumes that harm enters the system at the point of modeling, as though the problem begins only when an engineer selects a method or tunes a parameter. That view is too narrow. Bias often enters far earlier, at the level of data generation, collection, and labeling. Suresh and Guttag (2021) show that downstream harm can emerge across the machine-learning life cycle, from measurement and sampling to model development and deployment. Their analysis is especially important for public policy because it shifts attention away from the simplistic claim that one can just "de-bias the data" and solve the problem. Datasets reflect social arrangements: who is observed, who is ignored, which behaviors are recorded, what institutions decide to measure, and how categories are constructed in the first place (Selbst et al., 2019; Suresh & Guttag, 2021).

Barocas and Selbst (2016) make the foundational legal argument here. Automated decision-making systems do not need to encode overt discriminatory intent to generate discriminatory outcomes. They can produce disparate impacts because the data on which they rely embeds prior patterns of exclusion. Even where protected characteristics are removed, substitute variables may continue to carry their effects. A postcode can stand in for race; a job gap can stand in for disability or caregiving burdens; prior contact with law enforcement can stand in for neighborhood surveillance rather than actual propensity for crime. In this way, the algorithmic system inherits and reanimates past discrimination while presenting its outputs as efficient inference rather than social judgment (Barocas & Selbst, 2016).

The problem is compounded by uneven visibility. Dominant groups tend to generate the "cleanest" and most legible data because institutions have historically been built around them. Marginalized groups are often over-measured in punitive systems such as policing, welfare compliance, and debt collection, while being under-measured or made invisible in domains linked to benefit and opportunity. This asymmetry matters. An algorithm trained on over-policed neighborhood data will learn enforcement patterns, not inherent dangerousness. An algorithm trained on credit histories shaped by discriminatory access to banking will learn financial disadvantage as if it were individual risk. An algorithm trained on employment records from historically exclusionary workplaces will treat the past as the most plausible model for the future. These are not technical accidents; they are distributive consequences of how social life is recorded (Barocas & Selbst, 2016; Tucker, 2023).

Bias also emerges through choices about labels and proxies. A particularly revealing example comes from health care. Obermeyer et al. (2019) found racial bias in a widely used population-health algorithm because the system used health-care cost as a proxy for health need. That proxy appeared efficient from a modeling standpoint, but it failed normatively because Black patients had historically received less care and therefore generated lower cost data despite being sicker. The algorithm did not explicitly classify by race; it transformed unequal access to care into a misleading signal of lower need. This is precisely the kind of proxy error that makes algorithmic governance dangerous. A variable can be statistically convenient while morally and politically indefensible (Obermeyer et al., 2019).

This example reveals a broader lesson: the issue is not only biased data but biased institutional objectives. If a system is designed to predict cost rather than need, arrest rather than victimization, repayment rather than equitable access to credit, the resulting model may be highly accurate on its own terms while being deeply unjust in practice. Public institutions often embrace optimization because it appears apolitical. Yet choosing what to optimize is itself a political act. The algorithmic state masks that choice by displacing it into technical design (Obermeyer et al., 2019; Selbst et al., 2019).

FROM BIASED DATA TO UNEQUAL OUTCOMES

Once installed in institutional workflows, biased data does not remain static. It is converted into classifications, rankings, and thresholds that shape people's life chances. In employment, automated tools sort applicants before any human interview occurs. In housing, tenant-screening products assign risk scores to prospective renters. In health care, triage systems determine who receives extra attention and resources. In lending, complex models influence who receives credit and on what terms. The formal language may vary, but the social process is familiar: institutions classify people in ways that distribute opportunity and stigma unequally (Citron & Pasquale, 2014; Consumer Financial Protection Bureau [CFPB], 2023; Equal Employment Opportunity Commission [EEOC], 2024).

The employment context illustrates the point clearly. The Equal Employment Opportunity Commission (EEOC, 2024) has warned that AI and other automated technologies can affect hiring, promotion, training, pay, and termination decisions. The legal significance is substantial because employers cannot evade anti-discrimination law by outsourcing screening to vendors.

If an automated selection procedure has an unlawful discriminatory effect, the employer remains responsible. This matters because organizations frequently present hiring software as objective infrastructure rather than a contested employment practice. The technical veneer can thus shield routine exclusion from scrutiny, especially when candidates never learn why they were screened out (EEOC, 2024).

The same logic applies in credit markets. The CFPB (2023) has emphasized that lenders using AI or complex models must still provide specific and accurate reasons for adverse action. That guidance matters not as compliance advice alone but as recognition that opacity itself can become an inequality mechanism. If a borrower is denied credit through a black-box process and receives only vague or generic reasoning, the denial becomes difficult to dispute, correct, or appeal. In that sense, procedural opacity reinforces substantive inequality. Those with fewer resources and less technical literacy are least able to contest algorithmic judgments that may be wrong, incomplete, or unlawfully discriminatory (CFPB, 2023; Citron & Pasquale, 2014).

This is one reason why the algorithmic state tends to intensify existing inequalities rather than distribute error evenly. Mistakes are rarely random. They accumulate where data is thin, proxies are poor, and institutional stakes are high. Communities already subject to punitive surveillance or exclusionary screening are more likely to bear the burdens of false positives, over-classification, or denial. Meanwhile, privileged groups often benefit from cleaner data trails, more contestable decisions, and greater institutional presumptions of trustworthiness. Far from canceling bias, automation can regularize it (Suresh & Guttag, 2021; Tucker, 2023).

DIGITAL REDLINING AS COMPUTATIONAL SEGREGATION

The concept of redlining is indispensable for understanding inequality in the algorithmic state. Historically, redlining referred to the systematic denial of credit, insurance, and investment to neighborhoods marked as risky, usually because they were racially mixed or predominantly non-white. Contemporary law formally prohibits such discrimination, but digital systems can recreate similar exclusionary outcomes through data analytics, targeted marketing, geolocation, and personalized ranking. The key shift is from visibly drawn lines on a map to invisible classification systems built into platforms and models. What makes digital redlining powerful is precisely its opacity: exclusion can be personalized, probabilistic, and difficult to prove, while still reproducing spatial and racial hierarchy (Department of Justice [DOJ], 2022; Evans, 2019).

These civil rights challenges reveal how digital redlining reconstructs historical exclusion across the entire life cycle of economic opportunity. Upstream, digital platforms function as invisible gatekeepers; by optimizing ad delivery based on engagement patterns and proxy variables, they can steer housing and lending advertisements away from protected groups long before an application is ever filed (Department of Justice [DOJ], 2022; Evans, 2019). Downstream, the barrier shifts to opaque tenant-screening and credit-scoring algorithms. These systems routinely translate background vulnerabilities—such as address instability or prior legal contact—into automated risk scores that disproportionately burden Black and Hispanic applicants, tightening access through data-rich suspicion (DOJ, 2023). In both targeted marketing and automated screening, explicit demographic selection is unnecessary. Because variables like zip codes and browsing patterns act as proxies for race and class, the combined effect of platform design and background social inequality ensures that geography remains destiny. The explicit red lines of the past are replaced by probabilistic scores, allowing the old architecture of segregation to survive within the new infrastructure of personalization (Barocas & Selbst, 2016; Evans, 2019).

STRUCTURAL INEQUALITY AND THE RECURSIVE STATE

The deepest danger of the algorithmic state is not any single biased decision; it is recursion. Automated systems feed on the outputs of earlier institutions and then generate new outputs that become the data for later rounds of governance. Once a neighborhood is classified as high risk, it may receive more policing, more tenant screening scrutiny, worse loan terms, and less favorable insurance treatment. Those decisions then generate additional data points that appear to confirm the original classification. The system thus learns from the world it helps create. This is how structural inequality becomes self-reinforcing (Selbst et al., 2019; Suresh & Guttag, 2021).

Selbst et al. (2019) argue that fairness problems cannot be solved by abstracting a technical subsystem away from the larger sociotechnical context in which it operates. This point is crucial for governance. Public agencies and vendors often evaluate a model narrowly: Does it predict accurately on the chosen target? Does it reduce administrative burden? Does it improve detection rates? Yet those questions bypass the institutional system in which the model is embedded. A technically well-performing model may still intensify injustice if it operates inside unequal schools, labor markets, health systems, or housing regimes. The fairness question is therefore not simply whether the code works, but what kind of social order the code stabilizes (Selbst et al., 2019).

Tucker (2023) adds an important dimension with the concept of algorithmic exclusion. Sometimes inequality is reproduced not because the system sees marginalized people too clearly, but because it does not see them well enough to generate useable predictions at all. Sparse or missing data can leave people outside the domain of algorithmic legibility. New immigrants, the unbanked, low-income consumers with interrupted digital histories, survivors of domestic violence who deliberately reduce traceability, and people living on the margins of formal systems may all be poorly represented in datasets. Exclusion from prediction is not necessarily liberating. It can itself become a basis for denial, higher prices, additional scrutiny, or administrative friction. In this respect, the algorithmic state penalizes both hypervisibility and invisibility (Tucker, 2023).

This recursive structure also helps explain why entrenched inequality is so difficult to remedy after deployment. Once an algorithm is integrated into policy workflows, institutional incentives begin to align around it. Managers value speed and standardization. Vendors defend proprietary methods. Agencies become dependent on dashboards and scores. Front-line staff may defer to model outputs because doing so appears safer than exercising discretion. In turn, harmed individuals face steep barriers to seek review: they may not know an algorithm was used, may lack access to the underlying reasoning, and may encounter review procedures designed for bureaucratic paper errors rather than statistical inference. The process thus becomes self-legitimating (Citron & Pasquale, 2014; NIST, 2023).

WHY ANTI-DISCRIMINATION LAW STRUGGLES

Traditional anti-discrimination law remains essential, but it was not built for the full complexity of algorithmic governance. Much of modern equality law assumes a relatively identifiable decision-maker and a discernible adverse act. Algorithmic systems complicate both assumptions. Harm may emerge from proxies rather than protected traits, from optimization goals rather than expressed animus, and from platform-wide delivery processes rather than a discrete official decision. The causal chain becomes harder to narrate even when the distributive pattern is clear (Barocas & Selbst, 2016; Citron & Pasquale, 2014).

That difficulty has legal and political consequences. Organizations can claim that no one intended discrimination, that the software came from a third-party vendor, or that the system surfaced existing correlations. But disparate impact doctrine exists precisely because inequality often persists through formally neutral rules. What algorithmic systems add is scale, opacity, and speed. They can convert background disparities into thousands or millions of micro-decisions before oversight mechanisms can respond. This is why the Justice Department's interventions in housing and the CFPB's insistence on meaningful adverse-action explanations matter so much. They signal that existing civil rights and consumer law can still reach computational systems, even if doctrine must adapt (CFPB, 2023; DOJ, 2022; DOJ, 2023).

GOVERNING AGAINST ALGORITHMIC INEQUALITY

The policy imperative is therefore not simply to make algorithms more accurate. Accuracy is insufficient when the underlying target, proxy, or institutional context is itself inequitable. A more adequate response begins with governance principles. The OSTP (2022) argued in the *Blueprint for an AI Bill of Rights* that automated systems affecting rights, opportunities, and access to critical needs should be safe and effective, should protect against algorithmic discrimination, and should provide notice, explanation, and human alternatives. Even where the document is not legally binding, it articulates a constitutional and democratic intuition that should be axiomatic for the administrative state: people should not be quietly sorted into unequal life chances by opaque systems they cannot understand or contest (OSTP, 2022).

NIST's (2023) *AI Risk Management Framework* pushes in a complementary direction by stressing governance, mapping, measuring, and managing risk across the AI life cycle. Its value lies in rejecting the notion that risk is an afterthought or a public-relations add-on. In the context of inequality, serious risk management would require agencies and vendors to ask difficult ex ante questions: what is the target variable, and is it normatively appropriate? What proxy variables may encode race, class, disability, or place? Who is missing from the dataset? What error burdens will fall on which groups? And what pathways exist for review, correction, and appeal? Those questions move governance closer to democratic accountability and further from technocratic mystification (NIST, 2023).

Yet these governance mechanisms will fail if they are treated as box-ticking exercises. Inequality in the algorithmic state is not a problem that can be solved by adding a fairness metric to a dashboard. It requires institutional redesign: independent audits, public documentation, meaningful explanation duties, enforceable anti-discrimination obligations, data-quality scrutiny, and real human review for high-stakes decisions. It also requires a political willingness to say that some uses of automation are too harmful, too opaque, or too deeply biased to be legitimate in the first place. The key question is not whether the state should use data or prediction. It is whether public power can be exercised computationally without abandoning commitments to equal citizenship, due process, and democratic contestability (NIST, 2023; OSTP, 2022; Selbst et al., 2019).

The inequality produced by the algorithmic state is not incidental. It arises from the interaction of biased datasets, inappropriate proxies, opaque decision processes, digital steering, and recursive feedback loops. Bias in datasets yields unequal outcomes because data records prior inequality rather than transcending it. Digital redlining recreates exclusion through personalized ad delivery, tenant screening, and online credit marketing. Structural inequality is then reinforced when these systems are written into everyday governance and treated as neutral tools rather than political institutions (Barocas & Selbst, 2016; DOJ, 2022; DOJ, 2023).

For democratic theory, the lesson is stark. The algorithmic state does not replace social hierarchy with objective administration. It risks hardening hierarchy by translating it into code and scaling it through institutions that are difficult to inspect and even harder to hold accountable. The task, then, is not merely better engineering but a renewed politics of equality: one capable of asking who is seen, who is classified, who is excluded, and whose life chances are being quietly restructured in the name of efficiency. Until those questions are built into governance itself, the algorithmic state will remain a powerful engine for reproducing entrenched inequality.

Because the algorithmic state routinely converts historical patterns of exclusion into predictive scores and automated rankings, the civil rights response must operate before deployment rather than after harm. Algorithmic Impact Assessments should be mandatory for any high-stakes public system, requiring agencies and vendors to test for proxy variables and demographic disparities before a system is authorized—not as a compliance formality, but as a substantive gate on deployment. The Fair Housing Act and Equal Credit Opportunity Act should be applied aggressively to the algorithmic steering and ad-delivery systems of digital platforms, recognizing that upstream targeting decisions can discriminate before any application is ever filed (DOJ, 2022; DOJ, 2023). And civil rights organizations and collective entities must be granted legal standing to contest systemic algorithmic bias on behalf of affected populations, because the individualized injury model of traditional discrimination law is poorly matched to harms that are probabilistic, diffuse, and invisible at the level of the individual case.

6

DEMOCRATIC ACCOUNTABILITY IN A BLACK BOX SYSTEM

Prior analysis demonstrated both the limits of law in governing opaque systems and the ways in which those systems perpetuate structural inequality. The focus now turns to a prior institutional question: through what mechanisms is accountability evaded, and by whom? Where earlier discussion emphasized the distributive dimensions of the algorithmic governance crisis, this section examines the institutional pathways through which responsibility is diffused and obscured.

By dividing authority across the government, private sector, and artificial intelligence (AI), this hybrid state makes it nearly impossible to hold decision-makers accountable, which directly imperils a functioning democracy. Today, many consequential decisions are no longer made by a single identifiable official; instead, they are produced through interconnected computational systems—risk models, scoring tools, and automated workflows—that distribute decision-making across multiple actors and stages. If accountability is to remain meaningful in hybrid governance, it must operate through infrastructural constitutionalism—ensuring that systems themselves are designed to be explainable, contestable, and auditable.

A benefits denial may reflect an unseen data input, a model classification, and a procedural rule. A policing decision may be shaped by predictive software before any individual officer acts. An immigration case may be routed, flagged, or delayed based entirely on unseen computational processes. In these settings, accountability does not disappear, but it becomes exponentially harder to locate.

This chapter poses a key question for modern governance: when decisions are made through systems, who is responsible for the outcome? The answer is not obvious, and that uncertainty poses a direct threat to democratic principles of transparency, accountability, and contestability.

FROM OFFICIALS TO SYSTEMS

Because discretion has migrated upstream—from identifiable officials to system architects—the question of who bears responsibility for algorithmic outcomes is not merely theoretical. It has become the defining accountability problem of hybrid governance.

THE ACCOUNTABILITY GAP

This institutional transformation creates what can be described as an accountability gap. Consider a typical algorithmic decision environment: elected officials authorize the procurement of a system, public agencies implement it, and private vendors design or maintain it. Meanwhile, software engineers determine its underlying mathematical logic. When a harmful or erroneous outcome occurs, responsibility is severely fragmented across these multiple layers of involvement. Officials may claim they merely relied on expert systems. Agencies may point to the vendor's design flaws. Vendors, in turn, may invoke proprietary protections and trade secrets to shield their algorithms from public scrutiny. Engineers, the actual architects of the logic, are rarely subject to public accountability at all. Consequently, no single actor fully owns the decision.

This diffusion of responsibility is not a theoretical concern; it actively and negatively affects real-world outcomes. Individuals denied life-saving benefits, falsely flagged as security risks, or subjected to heightened administrative scrutiny often encounter systems that will not provide clear explanations for their outputs. As Pasquale (2015) vigorously argues, opacity in such systems is almost never accidental. It is often purposefully built into their design, whether for technical limitations, institutional self-preservation, or commercial intellectual property reasons. The result is a new form of governance in which power is demonstrably exercised, but not easily attributed to any one source.

ENGINEERS AS POLICYMAKERS

One of the most significant—and least visible—shifts in the algorithmic state is the rise of software engineers as implicit policymakers. In traditional governance, policy choices are made through legislatures, agencies, and courts, where they are fiercely debated, documented, and subject to public oversight. In system-based governance, many of those choices are written directly into design decisions: what statistically counts as "risk," which demographic variables matter, and how outcomes are mathematically ranked or classified.

These are not neutral technical choices. They reflect deep, subjective assumptions about fairness, efficiency, and acceptable societal trade-offs. The controversy surrounding criminal risk assessment tools illustrates this dynamic perfectly. Studies of systems such as COMPAS have shown that different definitions of mathematical fairness can produce vastly different real-world outcomes, particularly across racial groups. As Berk et al. (2021) note, the intense debates over these tools reveal the irreducible tension between statistical accuracy and normative equity. Yet these normative choices are often made completely outside traditional democratic processes, decided in private boardrooms rather than public hearing rooms. This raises a troubling question: when public policy is written directly into proprietary code, how is it governed?

COURTS CONFRONT THE BLACK BOX

Courts have begun to encounter these issues, though often indirectly and with limited technical vocabulary. In *State v. Loomis* (2016), the Wisconsin Supreme Court upheld the use of a proprietary risk assessment tool in criminal sentencing, even though the defendant could not meaningfully access or challenge the underlying algorithm that helped determine his fate. The court openly acknowledged the severe opacity of the system but instead treated it as one factor among many in the judge's overarching decision. In *Houston Federation of Teachers v. Houston Independent School District*, the Fifth Circuit reversed a district court dismissal in 2017, holding that teachers had adequately pleaded a 14th Amendment due process claim because the opacity of the proprietary Education Visualization and Analytics Solution (EVAAS) evaluation algorithm—which neither teachers nor the district could independently verify—prevented meaningful contestation (855 F.3d 483 (Fifth Cir. 2017)).

The district subsequently ceased using the system for termination decisions, illustrating that meaningful judicial challenge to algorithmic opacity is possible, but only when the underlying due process violation is sufficiently stark to survive dismissal.

These cases reveal exactly this paradox in concrete judicial terms. Courts are generally willing to tolerate algorithmic tools to maintain administrative efficiency, but they are aware that this technical opacity severely paralyzes the rigorous, independent judicial review now demanded in a post-*Chevron* landscape. The problem is not simply that the computational systems are complex. It is that their specific type of complexity can paralyze the ability of affected individuals—and the courts themselves—to understand and legally contest decisions.

TRANSPARENCY AND THE LIMITS OF FREEDOM OF INFORMATION ACT (FOIA)

In practice, the FOIA runs into hard limits in the algorithmic context. First, algorithmic systems do not fit neatly into the traditional, paper-based category of documents. Understanding a computational system requires access not just to lines of source code, but to the historical training data, the evolving models, and the specific operational context in which they are deployed. Second, much of this critical infrastructure is controlled by private vendors. Agencies frequently invoke trade secret exemptions to deliberately withhold system details from public view. Even when disclosure does occur, the sheer technical complexity limits its usefulness to the average citizen. Code alone does not provide meaningful transparency for most people—or even for many technical experts. The result is a troubling paradox: as governance becomes more data-driven and precise, it becomes less transparent and more shielded from the public eye.

THE PROBLEM OF EXPLAINABILITY

The black box problem not only obscures data but shields human operators from liability. In administrative law, agencies must provide intelligible reasons for decisions to enable review and appeal. Because machine-learning models operate through complex statistical relationships, officials can diffuse responsibility when outcomes are challenged.

Burrell (2016) identifies three distinct forms of algorithmic opacity that limit democratic accountability: intentional opacity, in which corporations or state actors deliberately conceal system logic to protect trade secrets or competitive advantage; technical illiteracy, in which writing and interpreting code remains a specialist skill inaccessible to most citizens and officials; and inherent machine-learning opacity, in which the mathematical optimization processes of algorithmic systems operate in high-dimensional space that fundamentally resists human-scale interpretation. Together, these forms of opacity make it difficult for agencies to provide the meaningful explanations that procedural fairness requires. The constitutional baseline was established across two foundational cases. In *Goldberg v. Kelly* (1970), the Supreme Court held that welfare recipients must receive a meaningful hearing before benefits are terminated. In *Mathews v. Eldridge* (1976), the Court refined the tri-part test into a flexible balancing test: the required level of process varies with the weight of the private interest, the risk of erroneous deprivation under current procedures, and the administrative burden of additional safeguards. Algorithmic opacity distorts all three factors at once—it leaves the private interest undiminished, raises the risk of erroneous deprivation by making the basis for decisions invisible, and allows agencies to overstate efficiency costs as a reason to withhold explanation. Without meaningful explanation, the constitutional right *Mathews* guarantees is weakened in precisely the cases where the stakes are highest. Algorithmic systems raise a direct question: can state decisions remain legitimate when responsibility is continually deflected?

EXPLAINABILITY IS NOT ENOUGH

In response to these deep concerns, researchers have developed various technical tools to attempt to improve explainability—such as feature importance metrics, interpretable models, and simplified algorithmic approximations. They provide only partial explanations rather than full transparency. More importantly, they do not resolve underlying questions of fairness, bias, or acceptable risk. Explanation alone does not guarantee accountability. A system may be explainable and still produce inequitable outcomes.

ACCOUNTABILITY IN A HYBRID SYSTEM

Accountability in the algorithmic state is not technical alone; it is institutional. Modern governance operates through a hybrid system where public agencies rely on private systems and decision-making is distributed across actors. Traditional accountability mechanisms—elections, legislative oversight, and judicial review—were designed for an entirely different administrative era. Adapting them requires forging robust new approaches.

Emerging proposals include the implementation of rigorous algorithmic impact assessments, mandatory independent auditing, far greater disclosure requirements, and retaining meaningful human oversight in the loop of decision-making. Each addresses part of the problem, but none resolves it alone. The deeper issue remains institutional: accountability must be rethought from the ground up for a system in which decisions are no longer made by a single identifiable actor.

DEMOCRATIC LEGITIMACY UNDER STRAIN

Democratic legitimacy depends on three principles: the people can identify who is making decisions, they can clearly understand how those decisions are made, and they have the power to respond through democratic participation or legal redress. Algorithmic governance complicates all three of these pillars. Responsibility is diffused across actors, while opaque systems limit both explanation and meaningful contestation.

These systems offer advantages—efficiency, consistency, and scale. The main question is how these systems can be governed to preserve democratic values.

REBUILDING ACCOUNTABILITY

The momentous shift to system-based decision-making does not eliminate accountability, but it forcefully transforms it. Power is no longer exercised solely through elected officials and formal institutions. It is quietly installed in data pipelines, predictive models, and digital infrastructure. This chapter has argued that accountability is currently fragmented across multiple actors, transparency mechanisms heavily struggle to keep pace with technology, explainability is a necessary but insufficient remedy, and democratic legitimacy depends entirely on adapting formal oversight to these new forms of invisible power.

When decisions are made through systems, where does responsibility lie? In the algorithmic state, the answer can no longer be the vendor who wrote the code, the automated pipeline that processed the data, or the frontline worker who blindly deferred to a screen. Responsibility must firmly remain with the sovereign state. Even as public administration distributes its functions across private infrastructures and opaque models, the constitutional duty to provide due process and equal protection is nondelegable. Acknowledging that the state retains ultimate responsibility for its technological proxies is the necessary first step toward reclaiming democratic control. That challenge will undoubtedly shape the future of modern governance, leading directly to the next critical question: if accountability is changing in kind, how must the law realistically change to keep up?

Because this hybrid state fractures accountability across public agencies, private vendors, and automated decision logic, the sovereign state must actively reclaim rather than passively inherit responsibility for its technological proxies. Government agencies must retain ultimate liability for the systems they deploy and cannot transfer that responsibility to private vendors through contract or procurement architecture—the constitutional duty to provide due process is nondelegable regardless of who wrote the code. High-stakes automated systems must be subject to routine, independent technical audits conducted by parties separate from both the procuring agency and the developer, because self-assessment cannot substitute for external verification where conflicts of interest are inherent. And any algorithmic system that affects liberty, property, or subsistence rights must be subject to meaningful human review before its output becomes binding—the efficiency rationale for automation cannot override the constitutional baseline that consequential decisions require a human being capable of being held accountable. The institutional design for each of these requirements is developed in the final chapter's oversight architecture.

7

THE FUTURE OF AMERICAN GOVERNANCE: RECLAIMING DEMOCRATIC CONTROL IN THE HYBRID STATE

If the traditional map of American government begins with Congress, the presidency, and the courts, the map that emerges from this book looks significantly more complicated. The familiar institutions remain. Laws are still written, enforced, and interpreted; elections still organize political competition; and courts still resolve disputes. But these institutions no longer operate alone. Across the system, decisions are shaped by processes that are not fully visible within the constitutional order. A voter's information environment is curated by a platform. A benefits decision is structured by a data system. A policing strategy is informed by predictive models. A campaign message is tailored through behavioral analytics.

These are not peripheral developments; they are central to how governance functions. The result is not a replacement of American government but rather a fundamental transformation into something layered and interdependent—a system in which authority is shared across public institutions, private digital infrastructures, and computational processes. We have established that this paradigm shift strains traditional democratic principles, fragments the public sphere, operationalizes structural inequality, and creates an accountability gap. The algorithmic state does not merely assist traditional institutions; it reconfigures them, shifting discretion from visible frontline workers to invisible system architectures.

The task now is not to further diagnose the problem, but to design the institutional and legal architecture required to solve it. Reverting to a pre-digital administrative state is neither possible nor desirable. The computational systems that now mediate public life offer unprecedented capacities for scale, efficiency, and coordination. The defining task of the 21st century is, instead, one of democratic integration: how to harness the affordances of the algorithmic state without surrendering the constitutional commitments of due process, equal protection, and democratic accountability.

The argument developed in this book addresses first- and second-generation computational governance—rule-based systems and statistical machine-learning tools whose influence on administrative outcomes, while often opaque, is in principle traceable to a discrete act of procurement or deployment. The next frontier is qualitatively different. Autonomous artificial intelligence (AI) agents—systems capable not merely of recommending but of initiating, delegating, and completing multi-step administrative tasks without a discrete human decision point—threaten to dissolve the "material influence" standard this book develops in the due process chapter, because agentic systems may produce legally consequential outcomes through cascades of micro-actions that no individual actor expressly authorized and that no existing audit mechanism is designed to capture (Russell, 2019; Wooldridge, 2009). Their governance implications are most acute in precisely the domains the Digital Administrative Procedure Act (D-APA) proposal is designed to address: federal procurement, benefits adjudication, and law enforcement. Extending that proposal to encompass agentic architectures—by requiring agencies to define the scope of delegated authority before deployment rather than tracing harm ex post facto—is the most urgent unfinished task of the administrative reform agenda this book proposes.

THE ARCHITECTURE OF THE HYBRID STATE

To govern this hybrid state, we must first accurately define its architecture. The three pillars of the hybrid state mapped in this book's Introduction—public constitutional authority, private infrastructural power, and automated decision-making—do not operate as separate domains. They have fused. The issue this book has traced is how to reimpose democratic accountability across all three simultaneously.

Individually, each of these forms of power is familiar. Together, they create a new governance paradigm. Government agencies rely on privately developed systems to carry out sovereign public functions. Private platforms regulate speech and political visibility at a scale unmatched by traditional public institutions. Automated tools organize decision-making in ways that are often entirely invisible to those affected by them. Authority is no longer concentrated in identifiable offices; it is distributed across complex socio-technical networks.

To grasp the magnitude of this shift, one must contrast it with the original logic of public administration. The trajectory traced in this book—from Weber's rule-bound bureaucrats, through Lipsky's street-level discretion, to Bovens and Zouridis's system-level pipelines—now terminates in a governance architecture whose rules are written not by legislators or officials but by algorithms, and whose accountability mechanisms have not kept pace with that transformation.

Rather than occurring at the moment of human decision, discretion is embedded much earlier—in the foundational design of the system. Choices about what data to harvest, which variables to weigh, and how models are constructed determine outcomes in ways that are rarely visible to end users. This effectively redistributes power from frontline officials to private system designers and institutional administrators.

CITIZENSHIP, VISIBILITY, AND INEQUALITY IN A DATA-DRIVEN SYSTEM

As the architecture of governance changes, so too does the nature of citizenship. In the traditional democratic model, citizenship is defined through legal status and active political participation. Individuals vote, engage in public debate, petition their representatives, and are subject to laws. In hybrid governance, citizenship acquires an entirely new, passive dimension: data representation. Individuals are understood by the state not only as legal subjects possessing rights, but as data profiles—collections of attributes, tracked behaviors, and statistically inferred characteristics.

These digital profiles dictate how individuals are treated within both public and private systems: whether they qualify for housing assistance, how they are evaluated for criminal risk, what political information they encounter, and how they are targeted by campaigns. This redistribution of authority does not replace legal identity, but it adds a determinative layer through which governance operates.

A defining feature of data-driven citizenship is the weaponization of visibility. In a democratic society, visibility is usually framed as a political good—the ability to be seen, heard, and represented. In the algorithmic state, visibility is frequently a mechanism of control and exclusion. Marginalized groups are often heavily over-measured in punitive systems (such as policing, welfare fraud detection, and child protective services) while remaining entirely invisible in domains linked to opportunity and capital accumulation, such as prime credit lending and premium job recruitment (Eubanks, 2018). High visibility in hybrid governance often leads to increased scrutiny, administrative friction, and intervention. Conversely, "algorithmic exclusion"—where individuals lack the digital footprint required to be processed by a system—can lead to automatic denial of services (Tucker, 2023).

The digital redlining documented in Chapter Five—through which proxy variables such as zip codes and arrest records carry historical discrimination into algorithmic scoring—extends to citizenship itself, fracturing the democratic promise of equal treatment under law.

A POLICY BLUEPRINT FOR THE HYBRID STATE

Taken together, these reforms constitute a practical blueprint for infrastructural constitutionalism, translating abstract constitutional principles into enforceable design standards for algorithmic governance.

If this hybrid state developed gradually through the uncoordinated adoption of technology, democratic control must be reclaimed through deliberate, systemic reform. As established in the preceding chapters, twentieth-century accountability mechanisms—from *Chevron* deference to traditional antidiscrimination law—have not kept pace with the twenty-first-century distribution of algorithmic power. To resolve the accountability gaps across administrative design, platform governance, and civil rights, the state must build an anticipatory legal architecture focused on four critical domains of implementation:

SEQUENCING AND PRIORITIZATION: A THREE-PHASE REFORM ARCHITECTURE

Before turning to the specifics of each reform domain, a critical methodological point must be established: these reforms are not a flat list of simultaneous demands. They form a sequenced architecture in which some reforms are prerequisites for others, and in which the political conditions for later reforms must be cultivated by the institutional changes that precede them. Presenting them without sequencing invites the same failure mode that has plagued European AI regulation: formal requirements enacted before the administrative capacity to enforce them exists, producing compliance theater rather than structural accountability.

Phase I — Executive Action and Administrative Capacity Building (Months 1–18). The reforms in this phase require no new legislation. They can be initiated immediately through executive direction, Office of Management and Budget (OMB) guidance, and agency rulemaking under existing statutory authority. Priority actions include: mandatory publication of complete algorithmic system inventories across all federal agencies, translated into plain-language summaries accessible to affected individuals; operationalization of OMB M-25-21 into enforceable procurement standards that prohibit opaque-system purchases for high-stakes determinations (OMB, 2025); Federal Trade Commission (FTC) enforcement of Operation AI Comply principles as the baseline conduct standard for any AI system deployed in commerce (FTC, 2024); and an OMB directive establishing minimum staffing requirements—one technologist and one data scientist embedded on every regulatory team responsible for AI procurement or oversight, with these positions classified under a new Algorithmic Governance Specialist occupational series in the General Schedule (GS) pay schedule. These actions create the administrative fact pattern that makes subsequent legislation both politically feasible and technically credible: agencies cannot credibly defend their algorithmic systems in a post-*Loper Bright* environment if they have not first mapped and documented what those systems do.

Phase II — Legislative Foundation (Months 12–36, overlapping Phase I). Once agencies have built baseline epistemic capacity and Phase I audits have generated an empirical record of algorithmic system performance and failure, Congress is positioned to legislate on evidence rather than abstractions. The D-APA, the expanded Algorithmic Accountability Act, and the information fiduciary framework should be introduced as a coordinated legislative package—not as isolated bills that can be defeated piecemeal. The sequencing is deliberate: Phase I generates the administrative record that gives D-APA proposals credible empirical grounding, making them resistant to dismissal as speculative regulatory overreach. Phase II also establishes the federal floor that supersedes the current patchwork of state laws, transforming the 99–1 Senate vote from a defensive holding action into the foundation of a positive federal standard. Congress should resist the temptation to legislate comprehensively before Phase I is complete; premature legislation without underlying administrative capacity produces the kind of nominal compliance that characterizes the current landscape of agency AI governance (GAO, 2025).

Phase III — Institutional Consolidation (Months 30–60). The final phase creates durable institutional infrastructure designed to outlast any single administration. The Algorithmic Audit Authority—funded through vendor assessments and empowered with subpoena authority—becomes the permanent technical backbone of D-APA enforcement. Data trusts, chartered as independent civic entities with federal seed funding but governed by civil society boards, begin negotiating collective data agreements with platforms on behalf of the public. Judicial training programs administered through the Federal Judicial Center complete the institutional picture, ensuring that courts hearing D-APA enforcement actions possess sufficient technical literacy to evaluate algorithmic evidence without full dependence on party-appointed experts. This phase is the most vulnerable to political disruption and must be insulated through statutory rather than executive design wherever possible.

The dependency structure underlying this sequencing is not arbitrary. Phase II legislation without Phase I capacity-building produces exactly the compliance theater this book has documented: formal requirements that agencies satisfy through vendor attestations rather than independent validation, as the Texas Medicaid system demonstrated across a decade of Deloitte contract renewals (National Health Law Program et al., 2024). Phase III infrastructure without Phase II legislative authority produces audit bodies with no enforcement mechanism. And Phase I executive action without the long-term anchoring of Phase III is vulnerable to reversal—as OMB M-24-10 demonstrated when it was rescinded in April 2025 and replaced by a directive oriented toward acceleration rather than accountability (OMB, 2025). The three-phase architecture is designed to generate institutional facts at each stage—enforceable contracts, trained staff, empirical audit records, judicial precedents—that are harder to unwind than the executive order or legislative session that initiated them.

LEGISLATIVE REFORM (IMPLEMENTED BY: CONGRESS)

- *Enact a D-APA:* The Administrative Procedure Act (APA) of 1946 assumes administrative discretion is exercised by identifiable human actors whose reasoning can be documented in a static record. To govern machine-learning pipelines, Congress must enact a D-APA that establishes "dynamic rulemaking boundaries." Instead of approving a static algorithm, agencies must approve the optimization goals, acceptable error thresholds, and permissible data inputs. The D-APA must also codify a statutory "Right to

Contestability," mandating that any individual subject to an adverse algorithmic determination receives a human-readable explanation and a streamlined pathway for human error correction (Office of Science and Technology Policy [OSTP], 2022).

- *Expand the Algorithmic Accountability Act (H.R. 5511, 2025):* Congress must mandate Algorithmic Impact Assessments (AIAs) before systems are deployed to make critical decisions. Modeled loosely on the National Environmental Policy Act (NEPA), AIAs would force agencies to evaluate societal and legal implications before a technology is authorized. A credible AIA must require the agency to formally justify why an automated system is preferable to a non-automated alternative, detailing the specific trade-offs between administrative efficiency and procedural fairness.

The proposals above do not emerge from a vacuum. The European Union (EU) AI Act demonstrates that comprehensive ex ante algorithmic regulation is institutionally achievable: it establishes risk tiers, mandates conformity assessments for high-risk systems, and requires meaningful human oversight in domains affecting employment, credit, education, and law enforcement. European AIAs have proceeded further than their American analogs for identifiable reasons. The EU operates without a constitutional analog to the First Amendment's speech protections, which in the United States have been extended to platform content curation (*Moody v. NetChoice*, 2024). EU member states also share a regulatory culture that is generally more receptive to ex ante market intervention than the US tradition of notice-and-comment rulemaking and post-hoc judicial review. These differences explain why the legislative proposals in this section are calibrated to American constitutional constraints rather than imported wholesale from European models—but they also make clear that the goal of a governed algorithmic state is not aspirational. It has been partially achieved elsewhere, and American institutions can learn from that experience even where they cannot replicate it.

The international evidence is reinforced by domestic precedent. In the absence of congressional action, states have emerged as the primary laboratories for algorithmic accountability law. California, Colorado, New York, and Illinois have each adopted or proposed comprehensive rules addressing transparency, bias mitigation, documentation requirements, and sector-specific safeguards for automated decision-making systems (Ghosh et al., 2025). By 2024 and 2025, more than 1,000 AI-related bills had been introduced across nearly every state legislature (Ghosh et al., 2025), constituting the largest wave of sub-federal technology regulation in American history.

Colorado's Senate Bill 24-205—the Colorado Artificial Intelligence Act—is the legislative anchor of this movement. Enacted in May 2024, it requires deployers of high-risk AI systems, defined as those making or substantially influencing consequential decisions in employment, housing, healthcare, and education, to conduct annual reviews for algorithmic discrimination, provide consumers with notice and a meaningful opportunity to correct erroneous personal data, and offer human review of adverse decisions where technically feasible (Colorado General Assembly, 2024). Notably, Governor Jared Polis signed the bill while publicly expressing substantial reservations about its scope and implementation costs, calling on the legislature to amend the law before its 2026 effective date. This ambivalence from the bill's own signatory underscores a recurring tension in state-level algorithmic regulation: the gap between legislative ambition and executive confidence in a law's workability—a tension that the federal D-APA proposal in this chapter is specifically designed to resolve through clearer statutory boundaries and phased implementation mechanisms.

Illinois followed in August 2024, when Governor J.B. Pritzker signed HB 3773, amending the Illinois Human Rights Act to prohibit employers from using AI systems that subject employees to discrimination based on a protected class and requiring disclosure whenever AI materially shapes an employment decision (Martin, 2024). Illinois became the second state to impose such obligations, and legislation modeled on both Colorado and Illinois laws has since been introduced in Massachusetts, New Jersey, New York, Virginia, and Washington, D.C. (Martin, 2024).

These state-level developments cut in two directions for the book's argument. Affirmatively, they demonstrate that the core elements of the D-APA proposed above—impact assessment requirements, human review mandates, notice obligations, and discrimination auditing—are not aspirational. They have already been drafted, enacted, and are being implemented within American legal institutions, calibrated to American constitutional constraints. The goal of a procedurally governed algorithmic state is not aspirational at the domestic level any more than it is at the international one. What is missing is not the institutional model but the federal will to consolidate and universalize it.

- *Regulate Platforms as Information Fiduciaries:* Given these constitutional constraints, Congress must focus on regulating design architecture by treating platforms as "information fiduciaries" (Balkin, 2018). Despite critiques that traditional fiduciary law is an imperfect patch for digital monopolies (Khan & Pozen, 2019), this approach allows the state to hold platforms liable for the algorithmic amplification systems they intentionally design—such as the speed of virality or microtargeting—rather than the content of the speech itself.

THE PROCEDURAL MECHANICS OF THE D-APA

If infrastructural constitutionalism provides the theoretical justification for regulating algorithmic architectures, the D-APA provides the statutory mechanism. However, for the D-APA to function as more than a conceptual deterrent, it must articulate precise procedural rules that bridge the gap between static administrative law and dynamic machine learning. The core problem is temporal: traditional rulemaking moves in months and years, while algorithmic systems update in milliseconds. To resolve this, the D-APA introduces the principle of "dynamic rulemaking boundaries," operationalized through three specific procedural mechanisms: the codification of reviewable optimization metrics, a bifurcated notice-and-comment process, and a formalized statutory overlay to existing APA requirements.

(1) Translating Optimization Goals into Legally Reviewable Terms

The foundational requirement of the D-APA is shifting judicial review away from the impossible task of divining an algorithm's "intent" and toward the auditing of its mathematical boundaries.

Under current APA standards, agency actions are struck down if they are "arbitrary and capricious." The D-APA modernizes this standard for the algorithmic era by requiring agencies to translate their policy objectives into legally binding, quantifiable thresholds published in the Federal Register prior to system deployment.

Agencies cannot declare a mandate to "optimize for efficiency" or "maximize accurate sorting." Instead, the D-APA requires the publication of the algorithm's specific *objective function*, accompanied by hard statistical boundaries. These must include a maximum permissible *error rate* (e.g., a false-positive threshold that cannot be exceeded) and strictly defined *demographic parity constraints* to prevent disparate impact.

Once these metrics are codified, judicial review is transformed. An algorithmic system that drifts outside its established, publicly debated error thresholds is no longer just flawed; its continued operation becomes per se arbitrary and capricious under the law, providing a clear trigger for judicial injunction.

(2) A Bifurcated Notice-and-Comment Procedure
Subjecting every algorithmic weight adjustment to a traditional notice-and-comment period would paralyze the administrative state. Conversely, exempting machine-learning systems entirely strips the public of its right to participate in democratic governance. The D-APA resolves this through a bifurcated review system designed to accommodate the reality of dynamic model training.

- *Initial Deployment (Full Review):* The initial adoption of an algorithmic system requires a traditional, comprehensive notice-and-comment period. This phase is not focused on the black-box mechanics of the code, but on establishing the baseline optimization goals, approving the acceptable categories of training data, and setting the quantifiable error thresholds discussed above.
- *Algorithmic Updates (The Safe Harbor):* Once deployed, the system enters a "Safe Harbor" provision. As the machine-learning model ingests new data and updates its internal weights, no new public comment period is required—*provided* the system's outputs remain strictly within the legally established threshold bounds.
- *Accelerated Review and Threshold Breach:* If an agency wishes to alter the core objective function, or if routine audits reveal that the algorithm has breached its established error or parity thresholds, the Safe Harbor protections dissolve. This triggers an "Accelerated Review" process, forcing the agency to either suspend the system or initiate a new, expedited public comment period to justify the newly expanded parameters.

(3) Statutory Integration with APA § 553
A critical feature of the D-APA is that it does not repeal or replace the foundational APA of 1946; rather, it functions as a targeted statutory overlay to § 553, like the Regulatory Flexibility Act or the Paperwork Reduction Act—statutes that impose additional procedural requirements on agency rulemaking without displacing the APA's foundational provisions. Unlike those statutes, however, the D-APA's scope extends beyond rulemaking procedure to govern the procurement, deployment, and ongoing operation of algorithmic systems, making it a hybrid instrument: procedurally anchored in § 553 but substantively broader in reach. Its primary legal function is to close a pervasive loophole in modern administrative practice. Currently, federal agencies frequently deploy algorithmic

decision-making systems under the guise of internal "guidance documents," "policy statements," or "rules of agency organization, procedure, or practice"—all of which are exempt from § 553 notice-and-comment requirements. The D-APA explicitly closes this avenue. It statutorily redefines the adoption of any automated or algorithmic system that determines, adjudicates, or heavily influences individual rights, benefits, or privileges as a "substantive rule." By legally classifying infrastructural deployment as substantive rulemaking, the D-APA forces algorithmic governance out of the shadows of informal agency action and back into the procedural light of democratic oversight.

ADMINISTRATIVE REFORM (IMPLEMENTED BY: FEDERAL AND STATE AGENCIES)

- *Reverse Vendor Reliance via Procurement Standards:* The algorithmic state is the product of a specific political economy that hollowed out the administrative state, forcing a deep reliance on private technology vendors. When public agencies purchase proprietary algorithms, they outsource sovereign administrative discretion to vendors who routinely invoke trade secret protections to shield their code from public scrutiny (Pasquale, 2015). Agencies must weaponize procurement to forbid the purchase of fully opaque systems for high-stakes administrative determinations. Contracts must mandate full public access to training data and model architectures, requiring vendors to explicitly waive trade secret protections when systems adjudicate liberty, property, or subsistence rights. Specifically, every federal contract for an AI system used in high-stakes determinations must include three non-negotiable clauses. First, a *Performance Transparency Clause* requiring the vendor to provide, within 30 days of any written agency request, the system's training data schema, variable definitions, and a complete audit log of model updates in human-readable form. Second, an *Error Rate Accountability Clause* establishing the maximum permissible false-positive rate for the specific use case, with automatic contract suspension if that rate is exceeded for two consecutive quarterly audit cycles without a documented remediation plan. Third, a *Procurement Liability Clause* shifting to the vendor the costs of corrective action—including benefit restoration, appeal processing, and legal expenses—for any harm directly traceable to a documented system defect.

The Texas/Deloitte and Michigan Management Information and Data Analytics Strategy (MiDAS) cases both illustrate the consequence of absent contractual accountability: the state bore the full cost of remediation across years of documented failure while the vendor bore none (National Health Law Program et al., 2024; Michigan Department of Attorney General, 2022).

- *Build Epistemic State Capacity:* State capacity can no longer be measured solely by budgetary resources; it must be measured by epistemic independence. Agencies must transition from compliance-based to capacity-based governance by restructuring their workforces to embed technologists, data scientists, and algorithmic auditors directly alongside legal and policy teams. The minimum operational standard should be a 3:1 ratio of legal and policy staff to embedded technologists on any team responsible for procuring, overseeing, or adjudicating disputes involving algorithmic systems. Congress should create a new occupational series—Algorithmic Governance Specialist—within the GS pay schedule, with a career ladder and salary band comparable to that of federal information security officers under the Cybersecurity Workforce Assessment Act. Agencies should also establish mandatory validation cycles: every high-stakes algorithmic system in active use must be independently validated against its published optimization goals and demographic parity constraints within 12 months of initial deployment and every 24 months thereafter, with results published in the Federal Register as part of the agency's annual regulatory agenda. Agencies that cannot demonstrate compliance with these validation requirements should be presumptively prohibited from expanding their use of algorithmic systems into additional program areas until remediation is complete.

JUDICIAL REFORM (IMPLEMENTED BY: THE COURTS)

- *Establish Post-Loper Bright Review Standards:* The Loper Bright Opacity Paradox makes this requirement urgent: courts are now asked to evaluate algorithmic reasoning directly, without the shield of Chevron deference, yet agencies routinely deploy systems that cannot be explained. The judiciary must establish a presumption of unreliability for fully opaque algorithms used in high-stakes determinations. In a post-*Chevron* world, the burden of proof regarding the fairness, accuracy, and statutory compliance of an algorithmic system must lie squarely with the entity deploying it, not the citizen harmed by it. Courts should adopt a five-part threshold inquiry for any challenge to an agency action substantially shaped by an algorithmic system. First, has the agency identified, by name and version, the specific system that produced or materially influenced the contested determination? Second, has the agency published the system's objective function, error thresholds, and demographic parity constraints in a reviewable administrative record? Third, has the agency demonstrated that the system's outputs fell within those published thresholds at the time of the contested determination? Fourth, can the agency produce a human-readable explanation of why the system's output applied to the specific facts of the individual's case? Fifth, did the individual receive timely notice that an algorithmic system materially influenced their case, and a meaningful opportunity to contest the system's inputs before deprivation occurred? Failure on any of the first four prongs should trigger a presumption of arbitrary and capricious action under the APA. Failure on the fifth prong constitutes a per se due process violation under the tripartite *Mathews v. Eldridge* (1976) balancing test. This framework translates the Loper Bright Opacity Paradox into a concrete evidentiary standard: agencies that cannot answer these five questions have, by that failure, demonstrated that their algorithmic governance is constitutionally indefensible in a post-*Chevron* world.

- *Appoint Algorithmic Special Masters:* Judges cannot be expected to independently audit machine-learning models. The judiciary must expand existing practices under Federal Rule of Civil Procedure 53, which is already used in complex antitrust litigation (such as *In re Apple iPhone Antitrust Litigation*, 2011). Courts should routinely appoint "algorithmic special masters"—independent technologists and data scientists—to audit proprietary models, review training data, and translate technical findings into actionable legal insights for judges. An algorithmic special master should be presumptively required—subject to rebuttal only on grounds of case-specific impracticability—whenever: (a) an agency relies on a machine-learning model to make or substantially influence a determination affecting liberty, property, or subsistence, and that model is challenged in litigation; (b) a civil rights plaintiff alleges disparate impact arising from an automated scoring or classification system; or (c) a vendor invokes trade secret privilege to resist disclosure of a system's design, training data, or operational parameters. Qualifying special masters must hold credentials in both a computational discipline and a relevant substantive domain (law, public health, criminal justice, or social policy); must have no current financial relationship with any party to the litigation or their affiliated vendors; and must be selected from a standing roster maintained by the Administrative Office of the US Courts, modeled on the existing process for court-appointed scientific experts under Federal Rule of Evidence 706. The Federal Judicial Center should develop, within 18 months of D-APA enactment, a training curriculum on algorithmic evidence evaluation for sitting Article III judges, with completion required for any judge assigned to a district that hears more than 10 APA algorithmic challenges per calendar year.

INDEPENDENT OVERSIGHT (IMPLEMENTED BY: INDEPENDENT BODIES AND CIVIL SOCIETY)

- *Create a Centralized Algorithmic Audit Authority:* Congress should establish an independent federal entity, akin to a digital-era Government Accountability Office (GAO) or a dedicated sub-agency within the OMB, tasked exclusively with evaluating public-sector algorithmic systems. This body would provide agencies with the technical leverage required to push back against proprietary vendor claims and validate machine-learning models. The Authority should be constituted as a Type II independent agency—independent of the executive branch in its audit determinations, but with a Senate-confirmed director serving a fixed seven-year term—with a statutory mandate covering three functions: prospective review of high-risk algorithmic systems before federal deployment; concurrent monitoring of deployed systems through mandatory quarterly performance reporting; and retrospective investigation of algorithmic failures upon referral from any federal court, the GAO, or a petition signed by at least 500 affected individuals. The Authority should be funded through a vendor assessment—a fee charged to any company that sells or licenses an AI system to a federal agency, calculated at one-half of one percent of contract value—so that the cost of oversight is borne by the industry generating the need for it rather than by the general appropriations process, which makes the Authority structurally resistant to budget-cycle defunding. The Authority should have subpoena authority over vendor systems and training data and should publish its audit findings and any agency responses within 60 days of completion in a publicly accessible federal registry.

- *Develop "data trusts" and Civic Legibility:* Algorithmic harms are frequently systemic and probabilistic, requiring the introduction of "civic legibility." Civil rights organizations and labor unions must be granted legal standing to litigate against systemic algorithmic bias on behalf of their constituencies. Furthermore, governments should fund "data trusts"—independent civic organizations that pool collective public data and negotiate with platforms and vendors on behalf of the public interest, ensuring data is used to optimize equitable outcomes rather than solely for private corporate profiling. The legal standing mechanism requires specific statutory authorization: Congress must amend the APA to permit organizational standing in APA review proceedings for any entity that (a) represents, on a documented and ongoing basis, a population materially affected by algorithmic governance in a specific domain; (b) has submitted public comments in the relevant notice-and-comment proceeding or, where none was held because the agency improperly classified the system as a procedural rule, has filed a formal objection with the agency within 60 days of the system's deployment; and (c) can demonstrate that at least one of its members would independently satisfy injury-in-fact under Article III. This standard—narrower than an open public interest standing regime but broader than individual injury requirements—is designed to make systemic algorithmic bias litigable at scale without inviting undifferentiated public interest claims. Data trusts should be chartered with federal seed funding of no less than five million dollars per trust, governance authority vested in a board elected by the constituent population they represent, and a statutory mandate to publish annual reports on the data practices of any platform or vendor with which they negotiate, making these reports part of the public record accessible to the Algorithmic Audit Authority and to courts considering APA challenges.

THE INTEGRATED ACCOUNTABILITY ARCHITECTURE: HOW THE REFORMS DEPEND ON EACH OTHER

The four reform domains described above—legislative, administrative, judicial, and independent oversight—are not parallel tracks that can be built in any sequence or in isolation. They form a single load-bearing architecture in which each element is a structural dependency for the others. The D-APA creates the statutory obligation that transforms procurement standards from contractual aspirations into enforceable legal requirements: without it, vendor challenges to the Performance Transparency Clause will succeed in trade secret litigation because no statute compels disclosure. The Performance Transparency Clause generates the training data schemas, audit logs, and model documentation that give the Algorithmic Audit Authority something to independently review: without it, the Authority's findings will consist of vendor-supplied attestations rather than verified performance data, which is exactly the compliance theater this architecture exists to prevent. The Audit Authority's validated findings produce the administrative record that courts need to apply the five-part threshold test without full dependence on party-appointed experts: without that record, plaintiffs challenging opaque systems will lack the documented evidence of opacity that the test requires at the threshold stage. The Special Masters provision bridges judicial unfamiliarity until the Federal Judicial Center training curriculum reaches critical mass. Remove any single element and the others weaken in direct proportion.

Understanding the realistic failure modes is as important as understanding the design. Vendor consortia will resist the Performance Transparency Clause through trade secret litigation under federal and state trade secret statutes; that resistance is most likely to succeed before the Audit Authority is funded and before courts have adopted the five-part threshold test, because there is no institutional counter-pressure from either direction. The answer is sequencing: transparency waivers must be embedded in procurement contracts before vendors seek statutory shelter, establishing a contractual baseline that antedates trade secret claims. Congress may attempt to defund the Audit Authority through appropriations riders before Phase III is complete; the answer is the vendor-assessment funding mechanism—a fee charged as a percentage of contract value—which is self-financing and therefore structurally resistant to appropriations-cycle attack in ways that annually-appropriated agencies are not. Judicial unfamiliarity with algorithmic evidence will persist well beyond the first wave of D-APA enforcement actions; the Special Masters provision is the bridge mechanism that makes the five-part threshold test administrable before judicial training reaches critical mass. Each failure mode has a designed counter-mechanism, but only if the architecture is built in the correct sequence and those counter-mechanisms are treated as structural requirements rather than optional enhancements.

One threshold condition determines whether the entire architecture becomes viable, and it must be stated plainly: the integrated system works only if Phase I generates a sufficient empirical record of algorithmic failure—through mandatory system inventories, validation cycles, and audit logs—to make Phase II legislation both politically sustainable and judicially defensible. Without that record, proponents of the D-APA will face the same objection that has defeated every prior attempt at federal algorithmic accountability legislation: that the harms are speculative, that existing law is adequate, and that regulatory intervention is premature. The Texas Medicaid system and Michigan MiDAS failures documented throughout this book are proof of concept: both produced precisely the kind of evidence—documented system defects, quantifiable false-positive rates, vendor contract failures, harm trajectories traceable to specific procurement decisions—that Phase I inventories and validation cycles are designed to surface at federal scale (National Health Law Program et al., 2024; Michigan Department of Attorney General, 2022). The empirical record is not administrative preparation. It is the political and legal foundation on which the legislative and judicial elements of this architecture rest, and building it is therefore the single most consequential act in the entire reform sequence.

The integrated architecture described here will not be built in a single Congress or under a single administration. The case for it does not depend on that claim. It rests instead on a structural observation: each component, once established, generates institutional facts—procurement contracts with trade-secret waivers, a trained Algorithmic Governance Specialist workforce, judicial precedents on the five-part threshold test, Audit Authority findings in the public record, data trust charters negotiated under APA standing—that are substantially harder to unwind than the legislative session or executive order that created them. This is not optimism about politics. It is a claim about the stickiness of institutional design. The architecture is constructed to survive political reversal at any single phase because each phase creates facts that constrain what the next political moment can plausibly undo. That is the difference between a reform agenda and a wish list, and it is the reason this book's prescriptions are offered not as aspirations but as a sequenced institutional program.

CONCLUSION: RECLAIMING THE REPUBLIC

The automation of American government is not a historical accident; it is a choice driven by the pursuit of administrative efficiency, the commercial imperatives of the technology sector, and a persistent belief that complex social and political problems can be resolved through computation. The transition from street-level to system-level bureaucracy is therefore not merely an administrative upgrade—it is a rewiring of the social contract. This hybrid state constitutes the dominant architecture of governance.

Yet the efficiencies gained through algorithmic systems cannot be purchased at the expense of democratic visibility. Public administration must recognize data architecture itself as a site of political power. By building explainability, transparency, and contestability back into technological design, the state can ensure that automation enhances, rather than erodes, constitutional accountability.

A successfully governed hybrid state does not reject computational power—it domesticates it. In this reimagined republic, automated systems function as auditable public infrastructure rather than proprietary black boxes. Agencies possess the technical and epistemic capacity to validate the models they deploy, and courts are equipped to scrutinize algorithmic reasoning with the same rigor they apply to statutory text. Most importantly, citizens are treated not as data subjects but as participants in a legible administrative order in which the exercise of power remains reviewable and justified.

The *Loper Bright* Opacity Paradox may thus mark a constitutional inflection point: a reminder that the law's demand for reasoned decision-making cannot coexist with the state's dependence on unexplainable machines. We cannot demand justification from a government that has outsourced its reasoning process to code. Democratic legitimacy therefore requires a new synthesis—one that binds computational governance to the enduring principles of due process, equality, and public accountability.

The policy architecture proposed throughout this book—reversing vendor dependence, rebuilding epistemic state capacity, instituting algorithmic impact assessments, developing a *Digital Administrative Procedure Act*, and reconceiving platforms as information fiduciaries—illustrates one path toward such institutional renewal. These proposals are not a call for technophobic retreat, but for democratic mastery: the deliberate subordination of computational power to the rule of law.

The urgency of federal action is made concrete by the constitutional confrontation now unfolding over those state laws. The Trump administration's December 2025 executive order on AI established a national policy explicitly designed to limit state authority to regulate artificial intelligence (AI), creating an AI Litigation Task Force within the Department of Justice charged with opposing state laws deemed inconsistent with federal priorities (Ghosh et al., 2025). The order took specific aim at the Colorado Artificial Intelligence Act, asserting that the law's anti-discrimination requirements would "force AI models to produce false results"—a characterization that reframes the constitutional guarantee of equal protection as an obstacle to computational accuracy (Ghosh et al., 2025). The administration directed the Federal Communications Commission and the Federal Trade Commission to develop federal disclosure and conduct standards that would preempt conflicting state requirements.

That effort was partially checked—but only partially. In July 2025, the US Senate voted 99–1 to strip a proposed 10-year moratorium on state AI regulation from the budget reconciliation package known as the One Big Beautiful Bill Act, rejecting what had been a House-passed provision that would have suspended enforcement of over 1,000 state AI regulatory bills in exchange for federal broadband funding eligibility (U.S. Senate Committee on Commerce et al., 2025). The bipartisan breadth of the Senate's opposition—spanning conservative federalists concerned about state sovereignty and progressive consumer advocates concerned about AI accountability—reflected a congressional recognition that the absence of federal legislation cannot be resolved by preempting the laws that states have already enacted. Senator Marsha Blackburn, who co-sponsored the amendment to remove the moratorium, stated plainly that until Congress passes federally preemptive legislation providing equivalent protection, it cannot block states from protecting their citizens (U.S. Senate Committee on Commerce et al., 2025).

The 99–1 vote did not resolve the underlying constitutional question; it deferred it. The executive order's preemption strategy remains in place, and Senator Cruz has pledged to reintroduce moratorium legislation through a standalone bill. The battleground between federal deregulatory ambition and state algorithmic accountability is now the defining arena in which the questions this book has raised are being contested. It is the argument of this study that the hybrid state cannot be democratically governed through that conflict alone—through litigation, preemption battles, and executive order. It requires the deliberate legislative architecture this chapter has proposed: a Digital Administrative Procedure Act establishing federal standards for algorithmic transparency and contestability that set a floor rather than a ceiling, leaving states free to build upon them while ensuring that every American, regardless of state residence, is protected by the constitutional baseline of due process, equal protection, and reasoned administrative decision-making.

The future of American governance will not be determined by the capacity of AI, but by the adaptability of its institutions and the resilience of its democratic norms. The task, therefore, is not to retreat from the algorithmic state but to govern it—openly, accountably, and under law. We have mapped the hidden architecture of modern power. The next task is to reclaim it.

EPILOGUE: TEN PRINCIPLES FOR GOVERNING THE HYBRID STATE

TEN PRINCIPLES FOR GOVERNING THE HYBRID STATE

The United States is entering an era in which government decisions are produced not only by elected officials or civil servants, but also by algorithms, data infrastructures, and private platforms. This "hybrid state" can either erode democratic accountability or renew it, depending on how it is governed. The following 10 principles translate the book's findings into actionable guidance for policymakers, regulators, and civic leaders seeking to make technology serve democracy rather than the reverse.

1. Keep Humans Accountable for Machine Decisions

Automated systems may assist public agencies, but they cannot replace responsibility. Every algorithm used in government must have an identifiable public official answerable for its outcomes. Delegating to software never removes democratic or constitutional duty. Agencies should document who signs off on each system and under what legal authority it operates.

2. Make Algorithmic Processes Visible

Opacity undermines trust. Agencies and vendors must reveal the logic, data sources, and objectives of any automated system that affects people's rights or benefits. "Transparency" must mean useable disclosure—not just source code dumps but explanations in ordinary language that citizens and judges can understand.

3. Build Contestability Into Every System

Government by reasons means citizens must be able to question those reasons. Individuals who are denied services, flagged as risks, or targeted for enforcement through automated tools must receive notice and a clear route to appeal before harm occurs. Accountability requires mechanisms for reversal, not just explanation.

4. Audit for Fairness Before Deployment

Bias baked into data cannot be fixed after launch. Algorithmic Impact Assessments should be mandatory for any high-stakes public system, identifying potential disparate effects and proxy discrimination. Independent audits—not vendor self-assessments—should confirm compliance with civil-rights and due-process standards.

5. Treat Data as Democratic Infrastructure

Public data, like roads or water systems, is shared infrastructure. It must be maintained with openness, quality, and equity in mind. Government should support "data trusts" and civic intermediaries that let the public negotiate how data about citizens is used, rather than leaving it solely to private actors.

6. Regulate Design, Not Speech

In digital platforms and political communication, regulation should focus on *architecture*, not content. Law can constitutionally constrain how platforms amplify, target, or harvest data—without dictating what users may say. Structural, content-agnostic rules protect both free expression and public integrity.

7. End the Vendor Shield

When government relies on private code, it still bears public responsibility. Contracts must prohibit trade-secret barriers that block oversight. Vendors providing algorithms for welfare, policing, or adjudication must accept audit and disclosure obligations equal to those of agencies themselves.

8. Strengthen State Capacity for the Digital Era

Accountability depends on expertise. Agencies need technologists, data scientists, and legal analysts who understand machine learning and its risks. Public servants should be able to interrogate and, when necessary, override algorithmic tools—ensuring that technology supports policy goals rather than dictating them.

9. Modernize Administrative Law for Dynamic Systems

The Administrative Procedure Act of 1946 was written for paper memos, not self-updating models. Congress should enact a *Digital Administrative Procedure Act* that records how algorithms evolve, codifies a right to explanation, and ensures that updates undergo public notice like rulemaking.

10. Reaffirm Democratic Legitimacy in the Age of Code

Technology must remain subordinate to the Constitution. Efficiency cannot trump due process, equality, or transparency. Governing this hybrid state means building democratic values into the technical systems themselves—so every line of code used in governance answers to the public it serves.

For a consolidated implementation guide, see the appendix: actionable checklist for agencies and legislators.

CLOSING REFLECTION

This hybrid state is here to stay. Algorithms now sit beside bureaucrats, and platforms shape public life as much as legislatures do. These 10 principles chart a path for reclaiming democratic control without rejecting technological progress. If implemented, they would transform automation from a source of opacity into a new domain of civic accountability—where machines extend human capacity, but humans still define justice.

APPENDIX: ACTIONABLE CHECKLIST FOR AGENCIES AND LEGISLATORS

HUMAN ACCOUNTABILITY

- Identify a named official responsible for each automated system.
- Document statutory authority for system deployment.
- Require sign-off for model updates or threshold changes.

OPERATIONAL TRANSPARENCY

- Publish plain-language summaries of system purpose, data sources, and logic.
- Release model cards or equivalent documentation for all high-stakes tools.

CONTESTABILITY GUARANTEES

- Provide notice when automation shapes a decision.
- Offer a clear, timely appeal pathway with a human reviewer.
- Preserve all data and model outputs relevant to the individual case.

EX-ANTE ALGORITHMIC AUDITING

- Conduct Algorithmic Impact Assessments (AIAs) before deployment.
- Assess disparate impact risk using demographic and proxy-variable testing.
- Prohibit deployment if minimum fairness thresholds are not met.

DATA GOVERNANCE AS PUBLIC INFRASTRUCTURE

- Mandate data-quality standards for administrative datasets.
- Establish privacy-protective "data trusts" for civic oversight.
- Prohibit data uses that exceed the scope justified in an AIA.

PLATFORM GOVERNANCE (CONTENT-AGNOSTIC)

- Regulate amplification, targeting, and data-harvesting architecture—not speech.
- Require transparency about ranking and recommendation systems during elections.

END VENDOR SHIELDING

- Require procurement contracts to waive trade-secret defenses for audit.
- Impose liability on agencies for harms caused by vendor systems.
- Mandate full access to training data and performance metrics.

BUILD STATE CAPACITY

- Hire technologists, data scientists, and AI auditors inside agencies.
- Establish cross-functional teams (policy + legal + technical).
- Fund in-house model validation capabilities.

UPDATE ADMINISTRATIVE LAW

- Pass a Digital APA requiring:
- Dynamic rulemaking boundaries.
- Error-threshold publication.
- Public notice for major system updates.
- Retention of reviewable algorithmic records.

REAFFIRM DEMOCRATIC LEGITIMACY

- Require meaningful explanation for any system affecting liberty, property, or subsistence.
- Require that automated recommendations never be the sole basis for a final agency action in high-stakes domains.
- Ensure systems are designed to advance fairness, due process, and equal protection.

ABOUT THE AUTHOR

Dr. Nancy S. Lind is a Professor Emerita of Politics and Government at Illinois State University, where she served on the faculty for over three decades before retiring in 2021. She holds a Ph.D. in Political Science and Public Administration from the University of Minnesota (1985) and a B.S. from the University of Wisconsin–Stevens Point (1980). Since leaving academia, she has continued her contributions to the field as a nonprofit management consultant and holds multiple professional certifications in nonprofit leadership, fundraising, and financial management.

Dr. Lind is a prolific scholar whose research spans public administration, constitutional law, economic development, and governance. She is the author and editor of more than 20 books, including *Democratic Wealth Stewardship* (Emerald Publishing, 2026), *Corruption, Accountability and Discretion* (2017), and *Privacy in the Digital Age* (2015). Her work has appeared in journals including the *International Journal of Public Administration*, *Economic Development Quarterly*, and the *Social Science Journal*. She has served on the editorial boards of several peer-reviewed journals and has contributed chapters to numerous reference encyclopedias in public administration and political science.

A dedicated teacher and mentor, Dr. Lind received Illinois State University's Outstanding Teacher Award (2001), the CASE Professor of the Year Award (2004), and the Academic Impact Award from the Provost's Office (2021). She has chaired or mentored dozens of graduate students throughout her career and remains actively engaged in public scholarship and community service in Stevens Point, Wisconsin.

REFERENCES

Algorithmic Accountability Act of 2025, H.R. 5511, 119th Cong. (2025). https://www.congress.gov/bill/119th-congress/house-bill/5511

Angwin, J., Larson, J., Mattu, S., & Kirchner, L. (2016, May 23). Machine bias. *ProPublica.* https://www.propublica.org/article/machine-bias-risk-assessments-in-criminal-sentencing

Balkin, J. M. (2018). Free speech in the algorithmic society: Big data, private governance, and new school speech regulation. *UC Davis Law Review*, *51*(3), 1149–1210.

Barocas, S., & Selbst, A. D. (2016). Big Data's disparate impact. *California Law Review*, *104*(3), 671–732. https://doi.org/10.15779/Z38BG31

Bauserman, v. Unemployment Insurance Agency. (2019). *503 Mich. 169, 931 N.W.2d 539.*

Bender, E. M., Gebru, T., McMillan-Major, A., & Shmitchell, S. (2021). On the dangers of stochastic parrots: Can language models be too big? In *Proceedings of the 2021 ACM conference on fairness, accountability, and transparency* (pp. 610–623). https://doi.org/10.1145/3442188.3445922

Bennett, C. J., & Lyon, D. (2019). Data-driven elections: Implications and challenges for democratic societies. *Internet Policy Review*, *8*(4). https://policyreview.info/data-driven-elections

Berk, R., Heidari, H., Jabbari, S., Kearns, M., & Roth, A. (2021). Fairness in criminal justice risk assessments: The state of the art. *Sociological Methods & Research*, *50*(1), 3–44. https://doi.org/10.1177/0049124118782533

Bommasani, R., Hudson, D. A., Adeli, E., Altman, R., Arora, S., Bernstein, M. S. (2021). *On the opportunities and risks of foundation models* Preprint. Stanford Center for Research on Foundation Models. https://arxiv.org/abs/2108.07258

Bovens, M., & Zouridis, S. (2002). From street-level to system-level bureaucracies: How information and communication technology is transforming administrative discretion and constitutional control. *Public Administration Review*, 62(2), 174–184. https://doi.org/10.1111/0033-3352.00168

Burrell, J. (2016). How the machine "thinks": Understanding opacity in machine learning algorithms. *Big Data & Society*, *3*(1). https://doi.org/10.1177/2053951715622512

Centers for Medicare & Medicaid Services. (2024). *Medicaid and CHIP CAA reporting metrics*. U.S. Department of Health and Human Services. [Press release]. https://data.medicaid.gov/dataset/ebcfc16f-8291-4c61-82a4-055846d72f3a

Centers for Medicare & Medicaid Services. (2025). *CMS launches new model to target wasteful, inappropriate services in original medicare*. [Press release]. https://www.cms.gov/newsroom/press-releases/cms-launches-new-model-target-wasteful-inappropriate-services-original-medicare

Chamber of Commerce of the United States of America v. Environmental Protection Agency. (D.C. Cir. 2024). *No. 24-1054*. https://www.uschamber.com/cases/energy-and-environment/cerclarule

Chandrasekharan, E., Pavalanathan, U., Srinivasan, A., Glynn, A., Eisenstein, J., & Gilbert, E. (2017). You can't stay here: The efficacy of Reddit's 2015 ban examined through hate speech. *Proceedings of the ACM on Human-Computer Interaction*, *1*(CSCW). Article 31. https://doi.org/10.1145/3134666

Chevron U.S.A., Inc. v. Natural Resources Defense Council. (1984). *467 U.S. 837*.

Citizens to Preserve Overton Park, Inc. v. Volpe. (1971). *401 U.S. 402*.

Citron, D. K., & Pasquale, F. (2014). The scored society: Due process for automated predictions. *Washington Law Review*, *89*(1), 1–33. https://digitalcommons.law.uw.edu/wlr/vol89/iss1/2/

Colorado General Assembly. (2024). *SB 24-205: Consumer protections for artificial intelligence*. https://leg.colorado.gov/bills/sb24-205

Colorado Office of the State Auditor. (2023, September). *Medicaid correspondence: performance audit (report no. 2261P)*. Department of Health Care Policy & Financing. https://leg.colorado.gov/sites/default/files/documents/audits/2261p_medicaid_correspondence.pdf

Consumer Financial Protection Bureau. (2023). *CFPB issues guidance on credit denials by lenders using artificial intelligence.* https://www.consumerfinance.gov/about-us/newsroom/cfpb-issues-guidance-on-credit-denials-by-lenders-using-artificial-intelligence/

Corner Post, Inc. v. Board of Governors of the Federal Reserve System. (2024). *603 U.S. 799.*

Danaher, J., Hogan, M. J., Noone, C., Kennedy, R., Behan, A., De Paor, A., Felzmann, H., Haklay, M., Khoo, S. M., Morison, J., Murphy, M. H., O'Brolchain, N., Schafer, B., & Shankar, K. (2017). Algorithmic governance: Developing a research agenda. *Big Data & Society*, *4*(2). https://doi.org/10.1177/2053951717726554

Department of Commerce v. New York. (2019). *588 U.S. 752.*

Department of Homeland Security v. Regents of the University of California. (2020). *591 U.S. 1.*

Department of Homeland Security. (2024). *2024 DHS artificial intelligence roadmap.* https://www.dhs.gov/sites/default/files/2024-03/24_0315_ocio_roadmap_artificialintelligence-ciov3-signed-508.pdf

Department of Justice. (2022). *Justice Department secures groundbreaking settlement agreement with Meta Platforms, formerly known as Facebook, to resolve allegations of discriminatory advertising.* https://www.justice.gov/archives/opa/pr/justice-department-secures-groundbreaking-settlement-agreement-meta-platforms-formerly-known

Department of Justice. (2023). *Justice Department files statement of interest in Fair Housing Act case alleging unlawful algorithm-based tenant screening practices.* United States Department of Justice. https://www.justice.gov/archives/opa/pr/justice-department-files-statement-interest-fair-housing-act-case-alleging-unlawful-algorithm

Equal Employment Opportunity Commission. (2024). *Employment discrimination and AI for workers.* U.S. Equal Employment Opportunity Commission. https://www.eeoc.gov/sites/default/files/2024-04/20240429_Employment%20Discrimination%20and%20AI%20for%20Workers.pdf

Eubanks, V. (2018). *Automating inequality: How high-tech tools profile, police, and punish the poor.* St. Martin's Press.

European Parliament and Council of the European Union. (2024). *[EU Regulation 2024/1689] Artificial Intelligence Act.* https://artificialintelligenceact.eu/

Evans, C. A. (2019). From catalogs to clicks: The fair lending implications of targeted, internet marketing. *Consumer Compliance Outlook, Third Issue.* https://www.consumercomplianceoutlook.org/2019/third-issue/from-catalogs-to-clicks-the-fair-lending-implications-of-targeted-internet-marketing/

Federal Bureau of Prisons. (2026). *PATTERN risk assessment.* U.S. Department of Justice, Federal Bureau of Prisons. https://www.bop.gov/inmates/fsa/pattern.jsp

Federal Trade Commission Act of 1914. (1914). *15 U.S.C. § 45.*

Federal Trade Commission. (2023a, December 19). *FTC charges Rite Aid with failing to protect Black, Asian, Latino, and women shoppers from harms of facial recognition surveillance.* [Press release]. https://www.ftc.gov/news-events/news/press-releases/2023/12/ftc-charges-rite-aid-failing-protect-black-asian-latino-women-shoppers-harms-facial-recognition

Federal Trade Commission. (2023b, December 19). *Statement of Commissioner Alvaro M. Bedoya, in the matter of Rite Aid Corporation.* [Commission statement]. https://www.ftc.gov/legal-library/browse/cases-proceedings/public-statements/statement-commissioner-alvaro-m-bedoya-ftc-v-rite-aid-corporation

Federal Trade Commission. (2024, September 25). *FTC announces crackdown on deceptive AI claims and schemes.* [Press release]. https://www.ftc.gov/news-events/news/press-releases/2024/09/ftc-announces-crackdown-deceptive-ai-claims-schemes

Fields-Meyer, A., & Hertel-Fernandez, A. (2024, October 11). *AI is threatening the social safety net.* The American Prospect. https://prospect.org/2024/10/11/2024-10-11-ai-threatening-social-safety-net/

Gerber, A. S., Green, D. P., & Larimer, C. W. (2008). Social pressure and voter turnout: Evidence from a large-scale field experiment. *American Political Science Review, 102*(1), 33–48. https://doi.org/10.1017/S000305540808009X

Ghosh, A. P., Saperstein, C. J., Rendar, M., & Obinna, D. (2025, December 19). *New executive order seeks to ensure a national policy framework for artificial intelligence.* Pillsbury Winthrop Shaw Pittman. https://www.pillsburylaw.com/en/news-and-insights/new-executive-order-national-policy-framework-artificial-intelligence.html

Gillespie, T. (2018). *Custodians of the internet: Platforms, content moderation, and the hidden decisions that shape social media*. Yale University Press.

Goldberg v. Kelly. (1970). *397 U.S. 254.*

Hersh, E. D. (2015). *Hacking the electorate: How campaigns perceive voters.* Cambridge University Press.

Houston Federation of Teachers, Local 2415 v. Houston Independent School District. (S.D. Tex. 2017). *251 F. Supp. 3d 1168.*

In re Apple iPhone Antitrust Litigation. (2011). *No. 11-cv-06714-YGR*. N.D. Cal.

Isaak, J., & Hanna, M. J. (2018). User data privacy: Facebook, Cambridge Analytica, and privacy protection. *Computer*, *51*(8), 56–59. https://doi.org/10.1109/MC.2018.3191268

Jasanoff, S. & Kim, S.-H. (Eds.) (2015), *Dreamscapes of modernity: Sociotechnical imaginaries and the fabrication of power*. University of Chicago Press.

Jhaver, S., Boylston, C., Yang, D., & Bruckman, A. (2021). Evaluating the effectiveness of deplatforming as a moderation strategy on Twitter. *Proceedings of the ACM on Human-Computer Interaction*, *5*(CSCW2). Article 381. https://doi.org/10.1145/3479525

Judicial Conference of the United States. (2025). *Rules of practice and procedure report.* https://www.uscourts.gov/sites/default/files/document/rules_report_for_sept_2025_jcus_session.pdf

Judicial Conference of the United States. (2026). *Rules of practice and procedure report.* https://www.uscourts.gov/sites/default/files/document/march_2026_rules_jcus_report_final.pdf

Kaye, D. (2019). *Speech police: The global struggle to govern the internet.* Columbia Global Reports.

Khan, L. M., & Pozen, D. E. (2019). A skeptical view of information fiduciaries. *Harvard Law Review*, *133*, 497–541. https://harvardlawreview.org/print/vol-133/a-skeptical-view-of-information-fiduciaries/

Kreiss, D. (2016). *Prototype politics: Technology-intensive campaigning and the data of democracy*. Oxford University Press.

Lipsky, M. (1980). *Street-level bureaucracy: Dilemmas of the individual in public services*. Russell Sage Foundation.

Liss, S., & Pradhan, R. (2024, September 9). *Errors in Deloitte-run Medicaid systems can cost millions and take years to fix*. KFF Health News. https://kffhealthnews.org/news/article/deloitte-run-medicaid-systems-errors-cost-millions-take-years-to-fix/

Loper Bright Enterprises v. Raimondo. (2024). *603 U.S. 369*.

Manhattan Community Access Corp. v. Halleck. (2019). *587 U.S. 802*.

Martin, G. (2024, August 19). Illinois enacts new AI legislation, joining Colorado as the only states regulating algorithmic discrimination in private sector use of AI systems. *Employment Law Worldview, Squire Patton Boggs*. https://www.employmentlawworldview.com/illinois-enacts-new-ai-legislation-joining-colorado-as-the-only-states-regulating-algorithmic-discrimination-in-private-sector-use-of-ai-systems-us/

Mathews v. Eldridge. (1976). *424 U.S. 319*.

Michigan Department of Attorney General. (2022, October 20). *State of Michigan announces settlement of civil rights class action alleging false accusations of unemployment fraud*. [Press release]. https://www.michigan.gov/ag/news/press-releases/2022/10/20/som-settlement-of-civil-rights-class-action-alleging-false-accusations-of-unemployment-fraud

Michigan Department of Attorney General. (2024, January 30). *Class action settlement approved by Court of Claims in Bauserman v.* State of Michigan Unemployment Insurance Agency Press release. https://www.michigan.gov/ag/news/press-releases/2024/01/30/class-action-settlement-approved-by-court-of-claims

Moody v. NetChoice, LLC. (2024). *144 S. Ct. 2383*.

Motor Vehicle Manufacturers Association v. State Farm Mutual Automobile Insurance Co. (1983). *463 U.S. 29*.

Napoli, P. M., & Caplan, R. (2017). Why media companies insist they're not media companies, why they're wrong, and why it matters. *First Monday*, 22 (5). https://doi.org/10.5210/fm.v22i5.7051

National Academy of Social Insurance. (2025, April). *Task force on artificial intelligence, emerging technology, and disability benefits: Phase one report*. https://www.nasi.org/wp-content/uploads/2025/04/Phase-One-Report-Task-

Force-on-Artificial-Intelligence-Emerging-Technology-and-Disability-Benefits.pdf

National Health Law Program, Electronic Privacy Information Center, & Upturn. (2024, January 31). *In the matter of Deloitte consulting LLP*. FTC complaint. https://www.upturn.org/work/upturn-federal-trade-commission-deloitte-complaint/

National Institute of Standards and Technology. (2023). *Artificial intelligence risk management framework (AI RMF 1.0)*. U.S. Department of Commerce. NIST AI 100-1. https://nvlpubs.nist.gov/nistpubs/ai/nist.ai.100-1.pdf

NetChoice, LLC v. Paxton, (2024). *144 S. Ct. 2383* (consolidated with Moody v. NetChoice, LLC).

O'Neil, C. (2016). *Weapons of math destruction: How big data increases inequality and threatens democracy*. Crown.

Obermeyer, Z., Powers, B., Vogeli, C., & Mullainathan, S. (2019). Dissecting racial bias in an algorithm used to manage the health of populations. *Science*, *366*(6464), 447–453. https://www.science.org/doi/10.1126/science.aax2342

Office of Management and Budget. (2024). *Memorandum M-24-10: Advancing governance, innovation, and risk management for agency use of artificial intelligence*. Executive Office of the President. https://www.whitehouse.gov/wp-content/uploads/2024/03/M-24-10-Advancing-Governance-Innovation-and-Risk-Management-for-Agency-Use-of-Artificial-Intelligence.pdf

Office of Management and Budget. (2025). *Memorandum M-25-21: Accelerating federal use of AI through innovation, governance, and public trust*. Executive Office of the President. https://www.whitehouse.gov/wp-content/uploads/2025/02/M-25-21-Accelerating-Federal-Use-of-AI-through-Innovation-Governance-and-Public-Trust.pdf

Office of Science and Technology Policy. (2022). *Blueprint for an AI Bill of rights: Making automated systems work for the American people*. White House Office of Science and Technology Policy. https://bidenwhitehouse.archives.gov/ostp/ai-bill-of-rights/

Parshley, L. (2025, February 22). The fight against the AI systems wrecking lives. *Jacobin*. https://jacobin.com/2025/02/ai-algorithms-government-services-trump

Pasquale, F. (2015). *The black box society: The secret algorithms that control money and information*. Harvard University Press.

Richardson, R., Schultz, J. M., & Crawford, K. (2019). *Dirty data, bad predictions: How civil rights violations impact police data, predictive policing systems, and justice* (Vol. 94, pp. 192–233). New York University Law Review Online. https://www.nyulawreview.org/online-features/dirty-data-bad-predictions-how-civil-rights-violations-impact-police-data-predictive-policing-systems-and-justice/

Roberts, S. T. (2019). *Behind the screen: Content moderation in the shadows of social media*. Yale University Press.

Russell, S. (2019). *Human compatible: Artificial intelligence and the problem of control*. Viking.

SEC v. Chenery Corp. (1943). *318 U.S. 80*.

Selbst, A. D., Boyd, D. H., Friedler, S. A., Venkatasubramanian, S., & Vertesi, J. (2019). Fairness and abstraction in sociotechnical systems. In *Proceedings of the conference on fairness, accountability, and transparency* (pp. 59–68). https://dl.acm.org/doi/10.1145/3287560.3287598

Skidmore v. Swift & Co. (1944). *323 U.S. 134*.

State v. Loomis. (2016). *371 Wis. 2d 235, 881 N.W.2d 749*.

Suchman, L. (2007). *Human-machine reconfigurations: Plans and situated actions* (2nd ed.). Cambridge University Press.

Suresh, H., & Guttag, J. V. (2021). A framework for understanding sources of harm throughout the machine learning life cycle. In *Eaamo '21: Proceedings of the 2021 ACM Conference on Equity and Access in Algorithms, Mechanisms, and Optimization*. https://doi.org/10.1145/3465416.3483305

Suzor, N. P. (2019). *Lawless: The secret rules that govern our digital lives*. Cambridge University Press.

Thaler, R. H., & Sunstein, C. R. (2008). *Nudge: Improving decisions about health, wealth, and happiness*. Yale University Press.

Tucker, C. (2023, February 2). *Algorithmic exclusion: The fragility of algorithms to sparse and missing data*. Brookings. https://www.brookings.edu/articles/algorithmic-exclusion-the-fragility-of-algorithms-to-sparse-and-missing-data/

Tufekci, Z. (2014). Engineering the public: Big data, surveillance and computational politics. *First Monday*, *19*(7). https://doi.org/10.5210/fm.v19i7.4901

U.S. Government Accountability Office. (2023). *Artificial intelligence: Agencies have begun implementation but need to complete key requirements.* Report No. GAO-24-105980). https://www.gao.gov/assets/gao-24-105980.pdf

U.S. Government Accountability Office. (2024). *Biometric identification technologies: Considerations to address information gaps and other stakeholder concerns.* Report No. GAO-24-106293). https://www.gao.gov/assets/gao-24-106293.pdf

U.S. Government Accountability Office. (2025). *Artificial intelligence: Federal efforts guided by requirements and advisory groups.* Report No. GAO-25-107933). https://www.gao.gov/assets/gao-25-107933.pdf

U.S. Senate Committee on Commerce, Science, and Transportation. (2025, July 1). *Senate strikes AI moratorium from budget reconciliation bill in overwhelming 99–1 vote.* [Press release]. https://www.commerce.senate.gov/2025/7/senate-strikes-ai-moratorium-from-budget-reconciliation-bill-in-overwhelming-99-1-vote

Weber, M. (1978). *Economy and society: An outline of interpretive sociology.* (G. Roth & C. Wittich, Eds.). University of California Press.

Weidinger, L., Mellor, J., Rauh, M., Griffin, C., Uesato, J., Huang, P.-S., … Gabriel, I. (2021). *Ethical and social risks of harm from language models* Technical report. DeepMind. https://arxiv.org/abs/2112.04359

Winner, L. (1980). Do artifacts have politics? *Dædalus*, *109*(1), 121–136. https://faculty.cc.gatech.edu/~beki/cs4001/Winner.pdf

Wooldridge, M. (2009). *An introduction to multiagent systems* (2nd ed.). Wiley.

MAIN INDEX AND CASE LAW INDEX

MAIN INDEX

CASE LAW INDEX

POLICY TOOLKIT INDEX

Printed and bound by CPI Group (UK) Ltd, Croydon, CR0 4YY

21/09/2026

14966034-0006